CHARGE!

Looking Back, Facing Forward:
5 Wise Words of Counsel

Joe Noland & Stephen Court

For information write:
The Salvation Army
USA Southern Territory
Literary Council
1424 Northeast Expressway
Atlanta, GA 30329

ISBN: 978-0-086544-065-4

Editor: Dan Childs
Cover Art: Whitney Houston
Printed in the United States of America

Dedication:

These pages are dedicated to all retired officers, past and present, whose legacy we all fight to advance.

Contents

Cover design by Whitney Houston. Whitney is a third-generation Salvationist. She was born in Albany, Georgia, in 1986. She trained in design and graphics in her college years. She entered The Salvation Army's Evangeline Booth College in Atlanta in 2013 and was commissioned in 2015.

Foreword

Every officer of The Salvation Army spends two formative years training to be an officer. In training garrisons around the world, 730 Days of spiritual and missional preparation culminate to produce an officer ready to preach the gospel of Jesus Christ and meet human needs in His name without discrimination. Those days are valuable, and they are to be anticipated and celebrated with joy and excitement.

This work by Commissioner Joe Noland and Major Stephen Court adds practical wisdom to the knowledge gained during 730 Days of training. All those who endeavor to be Salvation Army officers would do well to read these words and heed the wisdom closely. Years of practical and godly experience fill the pages that follow. My own soul is stirred as I resonate with each wise word, even after 45 years of active officership.

The words of Solomon are as true today as they ever were before: "*Listen to advice and accept discipline, and at the end you will be counted among the wise*" (Proverbs 19:20).

God bless you as you serve Him each day. May He find you wiser than He did the day before!

Commissioner David Jeffrey
USA National Commander

INTRODUCTION

By Joe Noland

wis·dom: Accumulated knowledge of life or of a particular sphere of activity that has been gained through experience (Encarta World English Dictionary).

shelve: 3. to dismiss or withdraw somebody or something from active service (Encarta).

Retirement is really a misnomer, isn't it? So is the term "active service," especially in Salvation Army circles. I'm as active and productive as ever (a seasoned septuagenarian at this writing), and my creative imagination is forever fertile. You do not shelve "accumulated knowledge and experience," nor do you turn it off like a water spigot; it keeps on flowing with two possible outcomes: down the drain or, like the water flowing through Hoover Dam, channeled into power – creative, productive energy.

Within the retired officer ranks is a vast Army array of "accumulated knowledge and experience." The purpose of this little book is to share a sampling that will, hopefully, open up the floodgates. So take note, you present and future Army leaders.

While we cannot change the past, this accumulated, collective generational wisdom can be channeled into the Army's future as a modern day continuation of the Apostle Paul's ongoing biblical counsel and charge to us through Timothy (paraphrased):

"Christ Jesus came into the world to save sinners, of whom I am chief. However, for this reason I obtained mercy, that in me first Jesus Christ might show all longsuffering, **as a pattern** to those who are going to believe on him for everlasting life … **This charge I commit to you,** *future Army leader*, according to the prophecies previously made concerning you, that by them you may wage a good warfare, having faith and a good conscience …" (1Timothy 1:15-19).

Or as beautifully paraphrased in The Message:

"Here's a word you can take to heart and depend on: Jesus Christ came into the world to save sinners. I'm proof – Public Sinner No. 1 – of someone who could never have made it apart from sheer mercy. And now he **shows me off** – evidence of his endless patience – to those right on the edge of trusting him forever… **I'm passing this work on to you**, my *future leader*. The prophetic word that was directed to you prepared us for this. All those prayers are coming together now so you will do this well, fearless in your struggle, keeping a firm grip on your faith and on yourself. After all, this is a fight we're in."

We asked each contributing writer to make this scriptural challenge foundational to his/her "Charge!" Each was instructed to pattern their contribution in one of the following ways:

1. If I were starting over
2. The five things I would do differently
3. Five words of counsel (expanded) I would give to a future leader on the eve of her/his Commissioning, or to any officer taking up the mantle of leadership, no matter how far they are along the way."

Throughout 50-plus years of officership, I've kept the following quote on my desk as a constant reminder: "God doesn't mind a little '*show* business,' so long as it gets the message across!" These pages are filled with a bit of purely motivated 'show-me-off' business, purposed to get his prophetic message across.

A Compromising Joe! (Part 1)

By Joe Noland

Several years ago, Doris and I visited The Salvation Army's cemetery plot in San Francisco, where the physical remains of her officer parents are laid to rest, along with many other sterling PTG Salvationists. While ambling through that vast section, reminiscing over the familiar names inscribed on each headstone, an unexpected wave of nostalgia and longing swept over us, bringing to mind the lyrics of this 1960s hit song:

Those were the days my friend
We thought they'd never end
We'd sing and dance
Forever and a day

We'd live the life we choose
We'd fight and never lose
For we were young
And sure to have our way

La La La La La…
Those were the days my friend, those were the days.

And the verses accompanying this chorus (paraphrased):

Once upon a time there was an Army,
Where we marched and beat a drum or two.
Remember how we sang away the hours,
And dreamed of all the great things we would do.

Then the busy years went rushing by us,
We lost our starry notions along the way.
If by chance I'd see you on the corner,
We'd smile at one another and we'd say…

(Go ahead, sing and la-la along)

Just today I stood upon that corner,
Nothing seemed the way it used to be.
In my mind I saw a strange reflection,
Was that aging person really me?

Abiding there in the cemetery, it slowly dawned on us, "We know more people resting here than we do alive!" *In my mind I saw a strange reflection, was that aging person really me?*

We felt a touch of melancholy as we stood among those great hearts, and the image of that revered open-air stand at Market, Powell and Eddy in San Francisco flashed through our minds.

We had marched to that corner with many of them, banners and bonnets waving, crowds gathering, fire-a-volleys echoing and souls kneeling at the drumhead. *Once upon a time there was an army, where we marched and beat a drum or two.*

From the cemetery, we hopped in the car and drove directly to that memorable street corner, still awash in nostalgia. To our utter dismay it was no longer there in the same configuration, the three corners now merging together into a modernized plaza. What a disappointment! Change is a scary thing. *Just today I stood upon that corner, nothing seemed the way it used to be.*

In many ways the new, modern plaza design is much more conducive to street meetings. The people are still there – beggars, shoppers and tourists – many waiting in long lines to board the Powell Street cable car for its scenic journey to Fisherman's Wharf. Many of them are lonely, longing and looking for life's answers, I'm sure. *Remember how we sang away the hours, and dreamed of all the great things we would do.*

There was a disheveled-looking man in the plaza passing out tracts, wearing a sandwich board, its bold lettering admonishing onlookers to, "REPENT OR GO TO HELL!" Alas! The Salvation Army is no longer there. *Then the busy years went rushing by us, we lost our starry notions along the way.*

As we paused there reminiscing, the ghosts of corners past

appeared fleetingly in our mind's eye: University and 43rd and Broadway and Horton Plaza, San Diego; Bristol and Edinger, Santa Ana; Hollywood and Vine (insert your own street-corner memories here). *Those were the days my friend, we'd thought they'd never end, we'd sing and pray, forever and a day.*

Looking back, what would I have done differently? I would have heeded the Apostle's two following charges more closely and carefully: "... do this well, *fearless in your struggle*, keeping a *firm grip on your faith* and on yourself." Unfortunately, there were too many times when I compromised these two italicized phrases (a compromising Joe) – resulting in The Salvation Army no longer being out there, uncompromisingly, as we once were.

Fear is the great compromiser and often results in a *loosened grip*. It was Franklin D. Roosevelt, who said during World War II, "All we have to fear is fear itself." The grip held firm, the faith maintained and the war won.

Our eternal struggle is beyond compare. It is estimated that 70,000 people will die TODAY and every day without hearing the gospel of Jesus Christ! Were I doing it over, I would be bolder in my approach toward evangelism and soul-saving. And I would most definitely take more risks. The "fear of failure" feeling (which has given me pause on many occasions) would be resisted even more vigorously.

So my charge to you going forward:

Fight fearlessly – “Fear not, for I am with you” (Isaiah 41:10)

Get a grip! (Fight faithfully) – “This is the victory that has overcome the world, even our faith” (1 John 5:4).

Reclaim the highways and byways contemporaneously, fearlessly, faithfully and victoriously. “After all, this is a fight we’re in!”

(Continued in Part 2)

Commissioners Joe and Doris Noland have served The Salvation Army as a team in three territories over a lengthy career. Growing up in Southern California, they were commissioned in 1965 as members of the Proclaimers of the Faith session, going on to serve creatively, riskily and faithfully in three territories: USA Western, Australia Eastern and USA Eastern, where they retired as territorial leaders. Still vibrantly active, shuttling between Hawaii and California, their vision and mission continues through, among other things, the planting of a Cyberspace Streetcorner Corps: www.themorerevolution.com (Compassion in Omnipresent Action).

To New Officers

By Lois Rader

I spent my last five years of active service as chaplain of a large girls' group home in Long Island. The 72 girls who lived and went to school there at any one time ranged in age from 12 to 18 and were assigned to us by the courts. Some were there all my five years. The challenge was great and rewards few, but I requested the appointment, and my heart still goes out to those many needy girls. Though I cannot speak from experience as a corps officer, being the wife of a Salvation Army officer doctor, my heart and involvement has always been in the corps – both overseas and in New York. So after 34 years of service as an officer I offer these simple words to new officers.

1 Let our ultimate goal as officers of The Salvation Army be to bring people to faith in Jesus

Let us never be ashamed of the name of Jesus. We can minister to all people regardless of their ethnic background or religious persuasion, but salvation is found in no other name. Though we can't coerce conversion or withhold compassion, we shouldn't lose sight of our ultimate goal. Paul asked the Ephesians to pray for him that whenever he opened his mouth he would fearlessly make known the mystery of the gospel. What a goal!

In our fundraising we sometimes focus on meeting people's physical needs – how many meals we have served, how many beds we have supplied – to get the widest support possible, but I believe God will honor our ministry when we do all in the name of Jesus.

2 Let us allow ourselves to be known and our homes open and welcoming

Jesus let himself be known to the most ordinary people by living with his 12 disciples night and day for three years. It can be a temptation to keep ourselves aloof from our soldiers and others, and it's true we can't tell all to all, but we should be available to people and express our sincere interest in them and their circumstances. People should be able to "read our heart."

When we were going through a very difficult time at the Wayside Home School for Girls, I asked the director, who was not a Salvationist, if I could pray with him. Afterwards he said to me, "You're the first Salvation Army officer I've gotten to know." (He had even seen me rather upset a few times!) I hope he saw Jesus in me.

3 Let our family be our priority and let our deepest desire be to see our children place their faith in Jesus.

When we went to India with our five children (number six was born there), we had decided to home-school them while they were young rather than send them to the boarding school 250 miles away. Right away I was asked by my superior how I could perform my responsibilities if I kept my children at home. I was aghast. "I thought they were my responsibility," I replied.

That could have been the end of my officership right there, but besides home-schooling ours and a few other missionary children, (beginning each school day with Bible study), my involvement included entertaining many overseas guests. Some stayed more than a month, teaching nurses Bible and English, working with Sunday school children, attending Home League and prayer times with the national officer wives. We can still work hard and do many things that include our own children.

I remember a frustrated officer mother coming to me when she and her husband were sent to DHQ while their children were young. She was expected to go into the city three times a week, often with a little one in tow, and return when school let out. I suggested that she and her husband ask to return to corps, which they did. Together they were able to meet the needs of their children. Anyway, I believe the corps is "where it's at!"

4 Let us not be afraid to partner with other Christians who share our mission.

In India my husband organized a united Christian rally in the new stadium in town. It was the first time the local churches had joined together. Many who attended accepted Christ as Savior, even among the Muslims and Hindus of the area, though some asked to remain secret believers for fear of reprisal.

While at Wayside, women came to me from nearby churches and asked if they could help minister to our girls. Some came for chapel services and some helped mentor individual girls. They were a strong support to me, especially in times of discouragement. In The Salvation Army we may have the clientele people want to minister to, and we can use the extra hearts and hands.

5 Let our daily time with God remind us whom we are serving – through The Salvation Army.

When Samuel Brengle was asked what his greatest temptation was, he replied that it was to let his own time with God slip.

If he did, he was beset by all kinds of temptations. At different times in my life my time with God has been at various times in the day, but I know that I need to meditate on the Scriptures and pray every day and not just grab a tidbit here and there. There are emergencies when that time gets squeezed out. But if Jesus counted time with his Father as important as food, how much more is the Word critical to our spiritual well-being?

I also need the encouragement and support of a small accountability group. I have usually been a part of a women's prayer group who help bear each other's burdens. Officership can be lonely, and we need a few trusted friends we can confide in and pray with and for. It will help us over the rough places that are bound to come.

I said once to my officer daughter, "I have always been able to find an outlet for my desire to serve God and people in The Salvation Army." True, some aspects of any appointment are less enjoyable than others, like paperwork or cleaning houses for the arrival of new missionaries. But such tasks keep us humble.

I never wanted position or title. Some must bear those heavy burdens. But I thank God for the privilege I have had in reaching many different people in his name that I would not have had except for officership in The Salvation Army.

Lois Rader grew up in a small town in New Jersey. She attended Asbury College, where she met The Salvation Army and her future husband, Herb. After their marriage in 1960, she taught 7th grade science in Cherry Hill, New Jersey, while Herb attended Jefferson Medical College in Philadelphia. Following his surgical training, they journeyed to the Salvation Army's oldest hospital in South India. Lois home-schooled their five children there and taught in the hospital's school of nursing. After 12 years in India, the family returned to New York and to appointments at Booth Memorial Medical Center. Lois taught at the SFOT, and served as chaplain of a residential facility for troubled girls. The Raders live in Floral Park, New York.

Five Standards to Live By

By John Bate

Leading up to our retirement on the last day of the century I was asked the same question on a number of occasions – "If you had the chance, would you do it all over again?" To me the question is as old as it is ridiculous! We don't have the chance to live life over again so what is the point of the question? In my boyishness I always wanted to answer, "No, no. I think I'd try something else," but I was sure the reply would have been misunderstood.

I have also heard this response to a similar question – "Yes, I would do it all over again, only I would do it better!" This, too, I find a little inane as it assumes we could live a life over again and seems to indicate that the one being questioned didn't do his best.

The truth of the matter is that we all try to do our best, at the moment, considering conditions and opportunities. Later we may reflect that we could have done better, but conditions and opportunities may have changed, even in five minutes. Two hundred years ago John Greenleaf Whittier wrote, "*For all sad words of tongue or pen, the saddest are these: 'It might have been.'*"

For me, that was no way to come to the end of 41 years of active service as a Salvation Army officer. So, my answer to this inappropriate question was always, "I can't do it over again – but it was great while I was doing it!"

I have to add, so is retirement.

This reflects an attitude without which I think life would be drudgery or, at best, just bearable. If I inherited anything from my father, it was "to enjoy what I was doing and to do it enthusiastically." There may not be anything particularly religious in this advice (for it was applicable when I was at university and also later in my work as an accountant) but it speaks to me about a quality of life and a responsibility to ourselves.

Now, moving on to what we believe is a holy calling – officership in The Salvation Army – this dictum put my ministry into a totally different category. This "high calling" deserved those same qualities that the rest of my life demanded.

What were the standards that I was taught to apply?

1 Enjoy your work and do it enthusiastically and with sensitivity.

Of course, enthusiastic people sometimes are the least sensitive! "It is good and logical for me, so it must be good and logical for you!" does not contain one ounce of reason but speaks of self-centeredness, if not arrogance and selfishness. Having said that, enthusiasm and sensitivity are qualities to be sought after within the framework of our own character and being. When I hear the shouts of enthusiastic support at a football match, I wonder about our lack of enthusiasm in the church. (Perhaps our sensitivity keeps us quiet! I have often wondered if we are shy about showing our enthusiasm for the things of God simply because of our misunderstanding of the true meaning of enthusiasm. In Greek, "enthusiasm" simply means "God within." It has nothing to do with shouting and hollering but joy and feeling in what we are doing, always thinking of others who may need our understanding or encouragement.)

2 I have always enjoyed study and treat my books as friends.

I have not read all the books in my library, but I know where to look when I need help or guidance – much like my friendships. And I trust that I am a "book" in the library of my friends. Just as I have friends with whom I have a difference of opinion in some matters, so I also read books with which I do not agree.

We do not have to believe everything we read – something I experience often by simply glancing through any newspaper. Serious study provokes our own understanding and enlightenment. Our beliefs of today should not be the same as they were 10 years ago. They should be deeper, more profound and maybe even more embracing.

3 If enjoying books is high on my list, so is enjoying people.

One of my problems as a young corps officer was that I enjoyed study and preparation so much that once I started in the morning I could sit at my desk all day. The other problem was I enjoyed visiting so much that if I started visiting early in the morning I could be doing that all day as well. My challenge was always "balance;" I heard a colleague say once, "Where there are people, there are problems." To be kind, perhaps he was just having one of those days. But if it were not for people we would not have any work. "People are our business" seems a little crass and earthy – but it is nonetheless a basic truth in The Salvation Army. Perhaps the easiest way to understand that idea is to constantly remind ourselves of our calling – "… *he who was a free man when he was called is Christ's servant* (1 Corinthians 7: 22) Reminding ourselves of that truth is never wasted time.

4 I can never be thankful enough that as Salvation Army officers we do not have to plan our future.

In business life we study and work for a promotion and maybe even the next, with an eye on the manager's job or managing director. As officers we do not plan for the next promotion but follow the advice of Paul to Timothy to "*study to show himself approved* …" I appreciate the NIV translation of the verse that encourages, *Do your best to present yourself to God as one approved, a workman who does not need to be ashamed and who correctly handles the word of truth* (2 Timothy 2:15). Perhaps our greatest challenge is to protect our dedication. I recall during our first years at International Headquarters I was responsible for the production of a series of Sunday morning broadcasts titled "Banners and Bonnets." Each Sunday by 9 a.m. more people had heard The Salvation Army with singing, bands and a message than would be heard throughout Britain all day. It was a marvelous and popular ministry which I enjoyed immensely, although I have never had to work harder in any appointment within The Salvation Army. One Friday morning, I was sitting in the production room at the BBC, preparing an upcoming program when the producer said to me, "John, why don't you come and do this full time at the BBC? We need your kind of organizing and administration." I knew in that moment that I had been in that appointment long enough. My dedication was to ministry, not arranging programs, even though for that time my appointment required me to arrange programs. There is a big difference – and I was grateful for the clarity of the point I grasped that morning. Strangely enough, within a month I was served with farewell orders from that appointment without anyone knowing of the proposition which had been made to me.

5 There is, in reflection, a great feeling of accomplishment in having fulfilled the required time of active officership.

While the Retirement Certificate is now hidden with files of old papers, which perhaps will never be read, it does record the completion of what we set out to do 41 years previously. Career change is a much-discussed topic these days, and it is propounded as a positive benefit in the working lives of many people today. The Army has been way ahead in the career change process since its beginning. Officers have been moved from preaching to administration and back to preaching and then to social work since the early days of the Army. It is perhaps not so much what we do but the fulfilling of the calling that brings that sense of spiritual accomplishment. The people we have touched and the programs we have administered have been the means of attaining that accomplishment.

The day comes. We receive that certificate and salute and say, "Thank you for providing me with the means of service and of fulfilling my calling." And here comes the next generation, equally dedicated and perhaps even more prepared and qualified. God bless them!

Colonel John Bate served as a Salvation Army officer in eight territories as well as at USA National Headquarters and International Headquarters. He was born in Napier, New Zealand, and attended Victoria University in Wellington before entering officer training in 1958. Most of his officership was spent overseas on missionary service and in leadership roles in South America West and South America East territories as well as the USA West. He also served as aide-de-camp and private secretary to Generals Arnold Brown and Jarl Wahlstrom. He and his wife, Valda, retired from active service in December 1999 and live in Clearwater, Florida.

Marked Urgent

By Wesley Harris

Some Christians are so laid back about soul-saving as to be almost horizontal. Evangelism is for "sometime;" revival can wait! But the movers and shakers of the Church have recognized that the need for revival has been urgent. They have also known that although revivals may be characterized by the gathering of crowds, they are really about individuals being won for God.

William Booth, the founder of The Salvation Army, was one who had "urgent" written all over his life.

My mentor as a young officer was retired Commissioner George Jolliffe who had been a private secretary to William Booth and had actually lived in his house. He spoke of the intensity and urgency of the General, who was not only concerned whether his soul-saving Army would continue long after he was gone but took every opportunity to challenge the unsaved whenever he met them. His saving passion for people reached out to the cab or engine driver, the fellow traveler or the person he met on the street.

Something of the same intensity throbs through Paul's letters to Timothy. Paul was aware of the hurrying and scurrying that took place before the emperor visited a city, and he wanted Christians to have a similar urgent zeal to prepare for the second coming of Christ and save the lost.

We might eavesdrop and listen to the great apostle as with great earnestness he says, to Timothy, *"I give you this charge: Preach the word, be prepared in season and out of season..."* (2 Timothy 4:2). Much more than a casual request or throwaway line, Paul's admonition carried something of the explosive power of his pent-up passion, and it still reaches people today.

As a 17-year-old, I was looking forward to a career in journalism but attended a session of youth councils. It would be nice to say that I was arrested by the sermon that was given, but it didn't happen like that. God led the wife of our divisional youth secretary to whisper, "What about you, Wesley?" That was all she said, but amplified by the Holy Spirit, it was powerful. The question reached my heart.

It was the turning point of my life, the end of my small ambitions and the discovery of my calling and destiny as a Salvation

Army officer. Had I known them at the time I could have echoed the words of the poet Rupert Brooke: "Now God be thanked who has matched us with his hour and caught our youth and wakened us from sleeping."

In his charge or parting command to Timothy, Paul made clear that his roles would be many and varied. He had to be prepared to rebuke, correct and encourage with great patience and careful instruction. This would be no "cushy number" or soft option and no task for spiritual wimps. In the Message paraphrase Paul's dying warning, based on his own experience, was, "You're going to find out that there will be times when people will have no stomach for solid teaching but will fill up with spiritual junk food."

Christian ministry can take all we've got and then some. It can be demanding and disappointing, but I know of nothing more fulfilling. Of course, the vocation will be as big as our vision and as large as we make it with God's help.

We live in what has been called the "me generation" when many are out only for what they can get. But, really, it is only as we learn to give that we learn to live. President Harry Truman said, "The time is ripe for an appeal not to self-interest but to the hunger for great living which lies at the heart of every man. What young people need is not the chance of getting something for nothing but the opportunity to give everything for something great."

It is said that there is no such thing as sacrifice if the cause is big enough. The hope of a movement like The Salvation Army may lie in young people who are prepared to forfeit the comforts of life in the well-padded ways of Western society and do it tough in the third world or the slums of our great cities.

My wife and I visited Brazil and saw the Army at work in favelas or shantytowns of unspeakable squalor and violence. There I was humbly proud to share with some young women officers who wanted only to live out their lives among the indescribably needy people of the slums.

I was privileged to spend some time at the Army's War College in Vancouver. It is situated in a district of unspeakable dereliction with decaying buildings, graffiti, drugs, broken bottles and broken lives. But young Christians are ready to spend a year or more living in flea-ridden rooms and identifying with very needy people. The posh name for this activity is "incarnational ministry," but in simple terms it means going where the greatest need is found and living and loving for Jesus' sake. These young people go in the spirit of William Booth, who said, "I don't care how near to the bottomless pit I go in order to save mankind."

A common expression nowadays is, "Get a life," and sometimes the connotation is that people should loosen up and go on a round of pleasure-seeking. But the essence of the call of Jesus points in a different direction and affirms that, paradoxically, it is as we lose ourselves in service that we discover what life is really all about. As we share in the urgent mission of our Lord, we enter into his joy.

Wesley Harris was commissioned from Cardiff Stuart Hall in the United Kingdom Territory in 1948. He and his wife, Margaret, served in the UK Territory and at International Headquarters, and he was chief secretary in the Australia Southern Territoty. He also commanded the Scotland, New Zealand and Canda territories.

A Worthy Life

By Carol Bassett

In preparation for the work and ministry that his disciples would have after he was no longer physically with them, Jesus prayed for them. He prayed for their protection, for their abundant joy and for their sanctification. Additionally, Jesus told them to wait for the promised Holy Spirit, who would guide, equip, empower and enable them to do the work he had called them to do. They were set apart for Kingdom work.

As a Salvation Army officer I have been called by God to do Kingdom work and gladly live in submission to the Lord. I give witness to the words of William James Pearson found in the SASB No. 255.

I'm set apart for Jesus, with him to ever stay,
My spirit he releases, he drives my foes away.
He gives full strength for trial and shields when darts are hurled;
With him and self-denial I overcome the world.

From my vantage point of looking back over many years, I thank God that as a child I accepted Jesus as my Savior and then as a teenager claimed this promise: *Trust in the Lord with all thine heart; and lean not unto thine own understanding. In all thy ways acknowledge him, and he shall direct thy paths* (Proverbs 3:5,6 KJV).

This Scripture promise has been a reality in my life, and I praise and thank God for his guidance and the gift of the Holy Spirit and his sanctifying power in my life.

In his book, "The God Moment Principle," Alan D. Wright wrote, "How you remember yesterday determines how you will live tomorrow." Because I know God has been faithful in the past, I know I can trust him for the future! Even now, as I look forward to the days that are to come, I am confident that God will be with me in days of joy and in days of sadness. I know his mercies are new every morning and that he will minister his grace to me each day.

Looking back as you are facing forward, my words to you are from my own personal journey with the Lord. I know that throughout the years God has guided me in establishing personal priorities for my spiritual growth and well-being. I know you will also be guided by the Holy Spirit as you seek his direction on your personal journey of obedience to God's calling. It is my prayer that God will abundantly bless you and make you a blessing as you are engaged in Kingdom work.

- Make your personal private time with God a daily priority. Study and meditate upon the truth of God's Word, spend time in prayer and enjoy intimacy with the Almighty. You will lead a very busy life, but you will receive daily guidance, strength and inspiration to keep focused on Kingdom business, ministry and growth in your personal experience with the Lord. *Come near to God and he will come near to you* (James 4:8a NIV).

- Endeavor to be humble and joyfully give God thanks and glory. Remember that it's not about you but about being available to the Lord and allowing God the Holy Spirit to work in and through you. *I planted the seed, Apollos watered it, but God made it grow. So neither he who plants nor he who waters is anything, but only God, who makes things grow* (1 Corinthians 3:6-7 NIV).

- Live a life of integrity in every area of your life. Enjoy God's blessings, be joyful and cultivate a positive attitude, and others will be influenced by your example of holy living.

Let the beauty of Jesus be seen in me,
All his wonderful passion and purity,
O thou Spirit Divine, all my nature refine,
Till the beauty of Jesus be seen in me.

- Continue to become better equipped to fulfill your calling by ongoing learning through reading and educational experiences. However, be careful not to become impressed by your own knowledge. *Do your best to present yourself to God as one approved, a workman who does not need to be ashamed and who correctly handles the word of truth* (2 Timothy 2:15 NIV).

- Value and respect all people. We have a relational ministry. Interact with others in a way in which they will see Christ in you.

We will work with each other, we will work side by side
We will work with each other, we will work side by side
And we'll guard each one's dignity and save each one's pride
And they'll know we are Christians by our love, by our love
They will know we are Christians by our love
(Lyrics by Carolyn Arends)

Several years ago I decided on my own personal mission statement. It is taken from the Word of God. … *that I may live a life worthy of the Lord and may please him in every way: bearing fruit in every good work, growing in the knowledge of God …* (Colossians 1:10 NIV).

And so I say to you: Be strong in the Lord, rely on God's provisions and enjoy God's blessings. Stand firm in your faith and secure in God's promises. You will never face a situation that exceeds God's grace! *And my God will meet all your needs according to his glorious riches in Christ Jesus* (Philippians 4:19 NIV).

His love has no limits, his grace has no measure,
His power no boundary known unto men;
For out of his infinite riches in Jesus
He giveth, and giveth, and giveth again.
(Annie Johnson Flint SASB #30)

I close with words of praise and thanksgiving to God for the reality of his goodness and grace to me.

You have made known to me the path of life; you will fill me with joy in your presence, with eternal pleasures at your right hand (Psalm 16:11 NIV).

Commissioner Carol A. Bassett retired in 2006 having served as National President of Women's Ministries. As an active officer, in addition to corps appointments, she served in the youth ministry, training, divisional and territorial leadership positions and at International Headquarters. Carol is a gifted artist whose chalk art ministry has been used of the Lord throughout her officership. Carol is a graduate of Asbury University and in retirement has served as the Home League secretary and is a faithful soldier of the Old Orchard Beach, Maine, Corps.

Lessons Learned Along the Way

By Harold Hill

We know the famous last words: "If I had my time over again, I'd…". But I probably wouldn't, or couldn't, even if forewarned. The person I was back then tried to do the best he knew how; the person I am now might try to do some things differently, but he wasn't around at the time. Still, five things I might have benefited from learning earlier are:

1 I need to sort out my own stuff first.

As the cabin crews' pre-takeoff spiel reminds us, we need to put on our own oxygen mask first before attempting to assist anyone else.

I pick up a certain amount of debris in the course of life's events, in my relationships with God, myself and others (including The Salvation Army). If I don't deal with this stuff, it will keep getting in the way of everything else I do, including my ministry.

Dealing with it is what the doctrine of holiness is about. One of the most cogent and practical toolkits is to be found in the Twelve Steps of Alcoholics Anonymous. For the convenience of anyone not familiar with these, here they are:

1 We admitted we were powerless over alcohol – that our lives had become unmanageable.

2 Came to believe that a power greater than ourselves could restore us to sanity.

3 Made a decision to turn our will and our lives over to the care of God as we understood him.

4 Made a searching and fearless moral inventory of ourselves.

5 Admitted to God, to ourselves, and to another human being the exact nature of our wrongs.

6 Were entirely ready to have God remove all these defects of character.

7 Humbly asked him to remove our shortcomings.

8 Made a list of all persons we had harmed, and became willing to make amends to them all.

9 Made direct amends to such people wherever possible except when to do so would injure them or others.

10 Continued to take a personal inventory and when we were wrong promptly admitted it.

11 Sought through prayer and meditation to improve our conscious contact with God as we understood him, praying only for knowledge of his will for us and the power to carry that out.

12 Having had a spiritual awakening as the result of these steps, we tried to carry this message to alcoholics, and to practice these principles in all our affairs.

Before anyone shies away from the word "alcohol," let me say that while we may not all have the alcohol, we all have the "ism." Another name for it is "sin." For those uncomfortable with "God as I understand him," does anyone have any other kind? And in case we're above this sort of thing, we do well to remember Paley's warning against contempt prior to investigation.

2 I need to be accountable to someone – other than, as well as, my line manager.

Ministry (including leadership and administration) is a team activity; lone rangers get into trouble. No social worker or counselor is considered "safe" without accountability; ministry is no different. Regular supervision, mentoring, spiritual direction

– whatever name we give it – is like preventative maintenance for a car: Regular servicing may save expensive repairs, or failure, down the road. There is a proviso, of course. To quote Alcoholics Anonymous, "We must be entirely honest with somebody if we expect to live long or happily in this world."

3 I can forget about looking for the silver bullet.

The way we have chased after every new guru and wizardry is reminiscent of Hosea's picture of Ephraim like a silly dove, fluttering between Egypt and Assyria. Some programs of church growth and other such "business models" have been more like Ponzi schemes, gobbling up our time, energies and resources but leaving us weaker and poorer than before. The Salvation Army's own systems might actually work if they're worked at. (I love the summary given by Commissioner Amos Makina: "Preach the Word; visit the people; always get a receipt!")

4 I need to practice servanthood ("servant leadership," if God chooses).

The issue of servanthood can be crucial in hierarchical, quasi-military systems, where the seductive nature of power creates a hazardous environment for the spirit. It calls for special vigilance to be able to live counter-culturally within those environments. Therefore, this is even more a matter of attitudes and about serving, rather than using, people. It means being there for people, rather than assuming they're there for the fulfillment of our particular vision. My father once told me, "At the end of the day, the only part of our work that may endure is what we have contributed to the lives of others."

The first edition of *Servants Together* in 2002 proposed guidelines for both structural and attitudinal aspects of servanthood in this way:

- Develop non-career-oriented leadership models.
- Dismantle as many forms of officer elitism as possible.
- Continue to find ways to expand participatory decision-making.
- Teach leaders to be servants by modelling it.

Most of us can't do much about these things on the macro level, but we all can on whatever level we find ourselves. Micah put it simply: "Deal justly, love mercy and walk humbly before God."

5 I need to keep my eyes on Jesus, the "author and finisher" of my faith – the one who began it and can bring it to completion.

Ironically, professional Christians especially need this word, as our occupation can delude us into thinking that going through the motions is living the life. As George MacDonald said, "Nothing is so deadening to the Divine in man as the habitual handling of the outsides of holy things." Other things and people can then become substitutes for the real presence of God and we end up living vicariously instead of authentically. Keeping our eyes on Jesus centers us in the right place.

Major Harold Hill is a New Zealander who trained as an officer in the UK Lightbringers session and worked as a teacher in Rhodesia-Zimbabwe. Returning to his home country in 1978, he served in corps, then as education secretary and in various other headquarters appointments before he and his wife Pat (who worked as a general practitioner in a medical practice serving the disadvantaged) retired in 2007. His publications include "Leadership in The Salvation Army: a case study in clericalisation" and "Te Ope Whakaora, The Army that brings Life: Documents on The Salvation Army and Maori 1884-2007." His contribution to "Charge!" was originally a talk to graduating cadets.

Answering the Call

By Bramwell Tillsley

On the eve of commencing your life's work, remember that first and foremost, the ministry is a calling. As it was said of the Old Testament priest, so it must be said of the New Testament minister. *No man takes this honor upon himself; he must be called by God* (Hebrews 5:4).

Jesus said, "*You did not choose me, but I chose you*" (John 15:16). Keep in mind, the call of God comes in a variety of ways.

1 Sometimes God speaks directly, in tones clear and unmistakable.

"*This is the way; walk in it*" (Isaiah 30:21). To Paul – "*Now get up and stand on your feet. I have appeared to appoint you as a servant and as a witness*" (Acts 26:16). But this is not the only way he calls.

2 God speaks in terms of human need, though the need is not the call, but rather the means used by God.

General Bramwell Booth wrote: "The great need of the world – its lost condition – is sufficient call for anyone who has the opportunity to respond."

In that general sense, every Christian is called and is in *full time service* (1 Corinthians 6:19,20).

3 But God has chosen you personally and given you the deep conviction that "this is destiny."

In the challenging days ahead, it is this sense of "call" that will serve as an anchor in the midst of the storm.

I would urge you, through prayer and the Word, to keep your own heart right. *Above all things, guard your heart, for it is the wellspring of life* (Proverbs 4:23). How tragic is the experience described in the Song of Songs 1:6: *They made me take care of the vineyards; my own vineyard I have neglected. Keep watch over yourselves and all the flock of which the Holy Spirit has made you overseers* (Acts 20:28). The order here is significant –"yourselves – the flock."

I would urge you to be a man/woman of the Word. The Word is the one thing God has specifically promised to bless. *So is my word that goes out from my mouth: it will not return to me empty, but will accomplish what I desire, and achieve the purpose for which I sent it* (Isaiah 55:11).

This challenge, of course, implies the constant development of your mind. E.F.Scott reminded us that "the failure of Christianity as a moral force is more often than we like to think due to no other cause than intellectual sloth." Bishop Oxnam added: "Our generation will not be led spiritually by people it cannot respect intellectually." Jesus himself said: *Love the Lord your God with all your heart and with all your soul and with all your MIND* (Matthew 22:37).

Of course, matched with our knowledge of the Word must be a knowledge of the world to which we are being sent. It has been suggested that we study with the Bible in one hand and the newspaper in the other.

In the High Priestly prayer (John 17), Jesus prays: *Father, "as you sent me into the world, I have sent them into the world."* (John 17:18). What do you understand by the "world" into which you are being sent?

In the Sprunt Lectures at Union Theological Seminary, Waldo Beach suggested our world is marked by three basic characteristics:

1 Anomi: No norm for behavior – no absolutes – no authoritative standard of right or wrong.

2 Anonymity: Man has lost his sense of worth – his identity. He is plagued with such questions as: Who am I? Why am I here? Where am I going? Do I really matter as an individual?

3 Alienation: Broken fellowship with God and man.

Facing such a world, do not neglect the ministry of encouragement. *Anxious hearts are very heavy, but a word of encouragement does wonders* (Proverbs 12:25 TLB).

Dr. Carl Jung suggested, "The central neurosis of our time is emptiness."

Mother Teresa added: "The biggest disease today is the feeling of being unwanted, uncared for, deserted by everyone."

How a word of encouragement is needed.

Many preachers, including Dr. F.B. Meyer, have indicated that if they had life to live over again, they would devote more time to the ministry of encouragement. It was D.L. Moody who reminded us that people have a way of becoming what we encourage them to be rather than what we nag them to be. We are in need of more leaders like Barnabas – "son of encouragement."

See that the flock of God is properly fed and cared for (1 Peter 5:2, Phillips). "Cared for" is perhaps best represented by the biblical metaphor of the shepherd. Again Jesus said, *"I am the good shepherd and know my sheep"* (John 10:14). The only way shepherding can be accomplished on any more than a casual basis is to do what Ezekiel did when he responded: *"I sat where they sat"* (Ezekiel 3:15, AV) This was not from an office with a computer. Is visitation too old-fashioned a term? I think not.

By the way, if this is getting a little heavy, don't neglect to develop a good sense of humor. Be ready to laugh at yourself as well as at situations over which you have no control. Beware of taking yourself too seriously. In this regard, don't limit your ministry by a fear of failure. We are in desperate need of more creativity. If a plan does not work, put it down to experience. No good leader will criticize you for trying.

Although most of you will work within a system that requires accountability, keep in mind your ultimate accountability is to God. Hopefully, it will be said of you, *"They watch for your souls as they that must give account"* (Hebrews 13:17).

I close by reminding you of Paul's charge to Timothy in 1 Timothy 1:12 -15. Here he speaks of "amazing grace."

1 Emancipating Grace: *Christ Jesus came into the world to save sinners – of whom I am the worst* (v.15).

2 Employing Grace: *He considered me faithful, appointing me to his service* (v.12).

3 Enabling Grace: *Christ Jesus, who has enabled me* (v.12 AV).

4 Exceeding Grace: *The grace of our Lord was exceeding abundant* (v.14, AV).

This grace is available to you. "And God is able to make all grace abound to you, so that in all things at all times having all that you need, you will abound in every good work" (2 Corinthians 9:8).

Blessings on your ministry!

When God's work is done in God's way, it will never lack for God's supply

– Hudson Taylor

General Bramwell Tillsley served at nearly every level of Salvation Army leadership. He was commissioned with the Sword Bearers session of 1955 out of Kitchener, Ontario. He served as a corps officer, training principal and divisional commander. He was appointed chief secretary in the USA South in 1985, as Australia Southern territorial commander in 1989 and as Chief of the Staff at International Headquarters in 1991. He was elected as the 14th General in July 1993 and retired due to health concerns in 1994. His wife, Maude, was promoted to Glory in 2014. General Tillsley resides in North York, Ontario.

On Starting and Finishing Well

By Barbara Van Brunt

One of the sacred privileges given to me as a Salvation Army officer in more recent years was to be able to pray with selected new lieutenants at the time of their ordination during the Service of Dedication on Commissioning weekend. I remember the emotion that filled my heart just prior to the last of these occasions shortly before entering into retirement. Somehow I wanted to impart to the new lieutenants all the great privileges and challenges that lay before them.

It became very symbolic to me. I was laying down the mantle of active officership, and they were just beginning their journey. The emotion within me rose high, though no one around me was even aware. I knew it would be an impossible task to put all the thoughts and feelings I was experiencing into a short prayer with those anxious new lieutenants.

So this has become my opportunity to even think through and

write down what I feel may be helpful to a future Salvation Army leader or any Salvation Army officer, no matter how far they may be along the way.

Intimacy with God

Your relationship with God is without a doubt what will keep you going in the right direction and functioning with his purpose – not yours – constantly uppermost in your thinking. A Salvation Army officer's life is full of involvements, activities and constant demands. All of those things are bound to distract us, and life can become an ongoing blur without purpose. Without true intimacy with God, we lose sight of what really matters to God. Chuck Swindoll, in his book "Intimacy with the Almighty," said, "Christ can become obscured in the dust of religious busyness."

In his booklet "My Heart, Christ's Home," Robert Munger writes about the different rooms of the heart. One of those rooms he called the "Drawing Room," which he later renamed the "Withdrawing Room." It sounded warm and inviting with a fire and comfortable furniture. There he met with Christ each morning and received all he wanted to give him to help make the most of his day. But he soon found himself busy and rushing about for weeks and even months at a time. But one morning as he was hurrying down the stairs, he noticed

Christ sitting by the fire in the Withdrawing Room. He went in and said, "Christ, have you been here every day, just waiting for me?" Munger's awakening spoke so clearly to my heart as a young officer and gave me a "visual" to help me see that as much as I needed this intimacy, Christ was longing for time with me as well.

Draw near to God and He will draw near to you (James 4:8). Our part in drawing near involves discipline, and it is our responsibility to provide some quietness where we can share our hearts with Christ.

Silence and solitude can be the means by which we allow God to lead us to true rest in him and a way in which he gives us meaning and purpose in the midst of the craziness of our everyday life. Mother Theresa has said, "We need silence to be able to touch souls."

May we long for such refreshment from our Lord each day so that we may fulfill the true calling which he has placed on our hearts as Salvation Army officers.

Relationships matter most

I remember going to an officers councils several months after our first child was born. There we were divided into three groups, men, single women and married women. In the married women's group, each woman was asked to share a problem. Many of the women said that trying to get all their ironing done was difficult, which most of you reading this cannot even relate to today! Perhaps they were presenting that as a concern to avoid delving into the real burdens on their hearts in front of this large group of peers.

Two highly-regarded senior women officers were leading our session. As we continued sharing the problems, many women in the room were crying. Meanwhile, we kept hearing laughter coming from the room next door where all the single women were meeting. I knew many of them had expressed a desire to be married, and we all thought the situation was pretty ironic.

The strong advice given to us that day was this: "You are first a Salvation Army officer. You may be fortunate to be a wife and a mother, but you are first a Salvation Army officer." I must admit that I felt very confused when I left officers councils that day. I have a husband and a six-month-old bouncing baby boy, but I am first a Salvation Army officer?

I believe with all my heart that our leaders were completely sincere and would never intentionally misguide us. But after trying to comprehend the counsel that was given to me that day, I decided that somehow I was different. I could do it all! I could be a "super-wife" and "super-mom," and a "super-Salvation

Army officer." If that is something you are thinking today, I want you to know it is all a myth – it cannot be done.

If God has given you a husband or wife, your relationship needs time and energy. Any marriage takes hard work and consistency, with lots of give and take, and officer couples are no different. In fact, officership presents other challenges as you work together and adjust that working relationship with each new appointment situation.

Communication is key. Do not allow anger and resentment to build up in you. *Don't let the sun go down upon your wrath* (Ephesians 4:26) because it will only go from bad to worse. Be very sensitive to each other's needs. Help each other with the family and household chores and with the ministry. Both your ministry and your marriage will flourish when you feel unconditional love from your spouse. Being married to a contented person is more fun than constantly dragging a partner out of the swamp of frustration and despair. Enjoy all the moments together to the fullest.

Children are a *heritage from the Lord* (Psalm 127:3). They need lots of our love and our time. I had the idea that if we loved all we did for the Lord and the Army that they would naturally love it too – but along the way I discovered this to be another myth. Of course, this can happen, but it is definitely not a certainty. Don't allow your work to consume you to the point that you lose the relationships that are dearest and most important to you.

Find a balance

Finding and maintaining balance brings me back to intimacy with God. It all fits together. Only God himself can give us the wisdom and guidance to find that balance. Many women have told me they feel guilty when they are home and doing things for their family, feeling as though they should be "working," and when they are at the office or doing Army work, they feel guilt-ridden about not spending time with their family members. Satan loves us to be in this state, as we are pretty much ineffective in either area of our lives. Such feelings can create a battleground of the heart and mind if we allow them to consume us. You can recognize false guilt as it often leads us to despair and will take away the peace that God wants to give us.

We can become sidetracked by pursuing our own well-intentioned plans that may not necessarily be what God wants us to do. How easy it is to become involved in our "God projects." My to-do list has taken over my life on many occasions through the years. Sometimes it takes a while to realize what is happening. But God has always been so faithful and so very patient, bringing me back to where he wanted me, helping me to find his purpose and restore balance to my life.

When we were divisional youth secretaries, our children were very young. We traveled with them most weekends all over northern New England, visiting the various corps. In those days we had Sunday evening meetings that began around 7:00, and we always did our best to be back to our home corps for those meetings. The children were usually exhausted and not excited about attending yet another meeting. I remember sharing that with a Christian leader at a conference I attended. He said, "Barbara, you know what you need to do? You need to go home on Sunday evening and play games with your children."

My answer was, "Oh, I can't. We have to attend the Sunday night meeting," and I honestly believed that as though it were a law written down somewhere. In retrospect, I wish I had followed his advice. It wasn't sacrilegious, and it made good sense.

I still reiterate that always giving our best to the Lord's work is important, but he also does not want us to be workaholics to the detriment of our own family. You need God's wisdom and leadership every day as you make such choices.

Love your people

It doesn't matter where you are stationed, there are always people God wants you to love. If you find yourself lacking in compassion, seek God and ask him to fill you to overflowing with all of himself that you may care for your flock with a heart of love. He will never disappoint you.

Be there for your people. Crises are happening every day in people's lives, and they often don't know where to turn. Rest in knowing that God will always give you all you need to minister to them.

Through my years of officership, I have realized over and over again that the Army has been called specifically to minister to some very special people that other churches cannot always reach. I began realizing that fact in our first appointment.

When we arrived there, we found out that a group of ministers had been trying desperately to reach the people in a very poor and depressed area of that little town of 4,000 people. They finally got some of the people to come to their churches, only to find that they were totally rejected by their congregations.

The people lived in a place called 9-Row, near the railroad tracks and very segregated from the rest of the town. When they attended The Salvation Army, they felt very much at home and accepted. So the town's ministers, feeling very defeated, decided to put a monthly allocation in their budgets to help the Army, because they felt that was one way they could help the people.

I remember being up in Waterville, Maine, one Sunday when a

couple was struggling to get their son, who was in a wheelchair, into the chapel. I could hear the hurt in their voices and see the pain on their faces as they told me about so many churches they had tried to attend, and were asked not to come back because their son, with his disability and illness, made distracting noises. But, they said, we have found a church home here. We are loved and accepted at the Army.

God has privileged us so much to be able to minister to the people of our corps and our communities. They are often a precious, fragile people who have had their hearts broken and their lives shattered in some way. They come to us searching for love, searching for God, and we have been chosen by God to point them to the Christ. Jesus has taught us by example how to tenderly minister in his name to his children.

Finish well

What does it mean to finish well?

A book on mentoring by Robert Clinton has helped me immensely through the last several years as I wrestled with that question. At the end of your lifetime, you are still enjoying an intimate, vibrant, close relationship with God. You are more conformed than ever to the image of Christ. You are demonstrating the fruits of the spirit in abundance. You will be able to look back and see God's faithfulness to you throughout your lifetime. There will be people who have been affected by your life so as to count for eternity.

But most of all, 'Finishing well' means you will be more in love with Jesus than when you first began your journey.

May God help us all to live our lives fulfilling his purposes so we will finish well.

Lt. Colonel Barbara Van Brunt served The Salvation Army in the USA Eastern Territory since her commissioning from the Heroes of the Faith session in 1964 until her retirement in 2007. She served, with her husband, Fred, as corps officers in the Western Pennsylvania Division for their first 10 years. The remainder of her appointments were on divisional headquarters, serving in youth work, League of Mercy and women's ministries. During her last 15 years of active officership, she and her husband served as divisional leaders in Northern New England and in Massachusetts. Barbara has four grown children and three grandsons and now resides in Massillon, Ohio.

Called, Chosen, Set Apart

By Mervyn Leach

1 Be sure of your calling

Yours is a very personal history. Yours is a story to be told. You have been saved by grace and indwelt by his Spirit, and you have been called, chosen and set apart for special work. Your life is a story that is still being written.

There must have been a certain time in a certain place when you were nudged or prodded by the Holy Spirit into giving ministry of the gospel and Salvation Army officership serious consideration. You found that you were compelled by love to respond and answer the call. There really was nothing else that you could do. This was, and is, God's will for your life. You've placed your all on the altar.

Yours is a most sacred trust. Let your integrity shine through in all that you do. Into your hands has been placed the care and keeping of a precious flock of people. You are responsible for their development and growth in the Christian way.

You must strive, as did the Apostle Paul, to be many things to many people so that you might win some. "The Message," referencing 1 Corinthians 9:21-23, reminds us that you and those like you are harvest hands and don't need any equipment. "You are the equipment," the text says.

2 Preach for a verdict

Keep your preaching simple. Make the message clear and plain. Communicate with such warmth and sincerity that the little old lady in the back row will feel that she's just been hugged. Be yourself. Use stories and good illustrations from life. Use even your own story.

Be diligent in study and preparation. Bathe your preparations in prayer. Go to God before you go to your people. Let the message speak to your heart first before you go to the pulpit to share it.

Work with themes. Make your meeting outlines support your theme. See that your theme flows to a conclusion and challenge that supports a call to commitment. If you fail to plan you will plan to fail.

Remember the old adage; "If you can't strike oil in 20 minutes, quit boring."

Do not neglect the Mercy Seat. It is unique to The Salvation Army. Make your invitation clear and plain. Never assume the entire congregation, large or small, is without the need to make a public confession of salvation or sanctification. Fight for souls with conviction and perseverance.

3 Pastor your people

This is an area sadly neglected in the present day and age.

Visit them in their homes. This is a valuable opportunity to meet your people on their own turf, where they can let down their guard and be open and frank as they begin to trust you and your level of confidentiality. With many of your people working, two to a household, it is more difficult to accomplish visitation, but it can be done by careful and prayerful scheduling, even during evening hours or over lunch or a coffee.

As trust grows, so does their willingness to open up many areas of their lives, especially the hurts that may have lain dormant for years.

Pastoral care of the flock helps you with preparing more appropriate sermons as you try to meet them at their point of need.

Be consistent in dealing with matters of discipline by carefully following the appropriate orders and regulations, making a level playing field and showing no partiality. Constantly study to make yourself competent to counsel. Never go beyond your level of competency. "Mow to the edges of your own field." Know when it is time to refer to the Christian professionals.

4 Be an encourager

Dale Carnegie, in his book, "How to Win Friends and Influence People," said, "Be hearty in your approbation and lavish with your praise." People will respond, not to flattery, but to well-earned praise.

Appropriate and sincere commendations go so much farther than constructive criticism, even though there are times when the latter is called for.

Nurture, mentor, disciple, teach and encourage, knowing that apathy in the pew can be contagious and negativity can spread like a prairie wild fire.

Do not neglect the hardened hearts and the antagonists in your ministry unit. A phrase, "Keep your friends close and your enemies even closer," can apply. Many a soldier saint has been won through dogged determination and persistence. The more they oppose and the more they question and argue, the more likely they are secretly searching for the truth.

5 Stay the course

Jesus said, in Luke 9:62, "*No one who puts his hand to the plow and looks back is fit for service in the kingdom of God.*" This text was given by a seasoned officer to a young candidate who was about to embark on a life of sacrifice and service, and that officer, after many years, attests to the marked impression that was made on his life and ministry.

Whether serving a congregation or administering in a social services setting, it is so easy, through the attacks of Satan, to become discouraged by circumstances, disappointed in people who let you down and dismayed by a lack of response. This will drive you to your knees more often than you will ever remember.

It was Robert Schuller, founding pastor of the great Crystal Cathedral in Orange County, California, who highlighted for me that, "When the going gets tough, the tough get going."

What a privilege is yours to minister to a group of God's children. As Winston Churchill said, "Never, never, never, give up."

A song in our song book, written by Anna Waring, puts it all in perspective:

Green pastures are before me
Which yet I have not seen;

Bright skies will soon be o'er me,
Where the dark clouds have been.
My hope I cannot measure,
My path to life is free;
My Savior has my treasure,
And he will walk with me.

Lt. Colonel Merv Leach, born and raised in Ontario, Canada, graduated from the Toronto training college in 1971 as a member of the Victorious session. He served in three corps appointments, on DHQ and training college staff and as divisional commander of three divisions. He retired in 2001 as the personnel secretary for the Canada and Bermuda Territory. He and his wife, Mary Belle, live in Brantford, Ontario.

They Will Know We Are Christians by Our Love

By John Nelson

I was born into a Salvation Army family. My parents were officers. My grandparents on one side of the family were officers and on the other, lifelong Salvationists. Nearly all my extended family are Salvationists, several of them officers. The Salvation Army culture was just about the only thing I knew growing up. The Salvationists around me, including my family, were so positive that I wanted nothing more than to become one of them.

When I was only 6 years of age I knelt at an Army Mercy Seat and asked God "to make me a good boy." When I was 13 and attending my first youth councils, I confirmed that I wanted to be a follower of Jesus in The Salvation Army. Having lived in a very active and enthusiastic Salvation Army officer home, I had no hesitation to positively respond to God's call to apply to become an officer when I was 17. I was commissioned before my 20th birthday.

When I was commissioned, I was convinced that the leading of God in my life and the will of my Army leaders was one and the same thing. When Elizabeth and I were married, little did we know what God had in store for us. By the time we retired we had spent over 30 of our 41 years of married service outside of Canada. Even in retirement, I have been asked on nine different occasions to take up appointments from six months to a year in various parts of the world. I praise God that I can say I have kept my commitment and have willingly accepted each appointment as part of his perfect will.

With all of the above, I believe I have the right to call myself a Salvationist. Over the years, particularly in retirement, I have had many opportunities to reflect on the years of our service, active and retired, and many of the thoughts and experiences we have had in many parts of the world. Yes, I see things differently today than I did when I started out. The world has changed tremendously during those nearly 60 years. The Army has changed tremendously too. My own spiritual journey has grown and matured and continues to do so to the present day. I thank God for that.

If I were starting over, there are several things I would approach differently, not because I was wrong when I started out, but because it was a different era altogether. Now, with the knowledge and experience of a lifetime and hopefully some God-given wisdom, I am what I am today by his grace.

Here are five issues I believe are important for leaders today:

1 If we are going to win the world for Jesus, we must live out the New Testament command to love God and our neighbor.

Jesus put God's love into practice and established a pattern that we must follow in every aspect of our lives, personally and corporately. We must accept that we can do so only by God`s grace and the empowering of the Holy Spirit in our lives. We must allow the fruit of the Holy Spirit – love, joy, peace, patience, kindness, goodness, faithfulness, gentleness and self-control – to be our authentic witness in all that we do and say. I see this as a significant and encouraging change in emphasis.

2 If we are going to win the world for Jesus, we must recognize that denominational, doctrinal, lifestyle and worship style distinctives are no more than boxes established throughout history.

Distinctives have become barriers that complicate our reaching out to the "whosoever" of the whole world in our quest to reach them for Jesus. I believe less emphasis should be given to distinctives and more focus placed on Jesus in order to fulfill his perfect will.

3 If we are going to win the world for Jesus, we must accept the fact that all Christians, wherever they are or however they express their faith, are part of the family of God.

We must work together with respect and humility and form partnerships whenever possible to communicate more effectively to the whole world the gospel of Jesus Christ. Traveling the world has caused me to see this as a more urgent need.

4 If we are going to win the world for Jesus, we must positively engage with all people within our community.

By doing that, we form the relationships and build the support that makes it possible for the Holy Spirit to bring about their faith in God and spiritual maturity. This engagement, often in practical terms, must begin with the individual.

5 If we are going to win the world for Jesus, we must go beyond our own faith and reach out to those of other faiths.

By respecting and engaging people of other faiths or those of no faith at all, we will learn what we have in common and what we can do effectively together. Our presence in their world will enable God to do his work in all our lives. Although such an outreach makes some people uncomfortable, this is an essential challenge.

If some of the above sounds radical, then so be it. Having traveled to many of the densely populated parts of the world and having lived in several countries where the Christian faith is a very small minority, I am convinced there is no more time for small talk, petty differences, greed, power struggles and jockeying for positions of so-called authority. We must set aside our differences and be united in the fundamental principles of God's love and together be witnesses of Jesus Christ. It is our task to witness as followers of Jesus and God's task, often through us, to bring about the salvation of the world and the establishment of his Kingdom.

Commissioner John Nelson is the son of Canadian Salvation Army officers. He experienced the call to officership during his teens and was a member of the Intercessors session commissioned in Toronto, Canada in June 1952. He served in the Caribbean for many years, and after serving in his home territory of Canada and Bermuda, John was appointed territorial commander of Pakistan. His final appointment was to IHQ as the international secretary for South Asia, which includes the six territories of India and territories in Pakistan, Sri Lanka and the Bangladesh Command. He retired in 1997 and lives in Winnipeg, Manitoba. His wife, Elizabeth, was promoted to Glory in 2016.

A Bit of Wisdom

By Claralyn Lowman

When my husband, Doug, and I were commissioned as corps officers in The Salvation Army, our responsibilities were right in line with the experience we had gained prior to training.

It had been quite startling to Doug's associates when they heard he would be leaving his job, although they were not really surprised to hear of God's calling him into full time ministry. They commented to me about his Christ-like interactions, genuine concern for employees, helpful counsel and ability to speak graciously in public on behalf of the employees. Doug had worked for over 12 years in a firm where he first handled employee records and finances, then progressed through various responsibilities to personnel directorship, along with mediating union/company arbitration, to directly assisting the CEO in the corporate office, and lastly, becoming vice president of administration. God had ensured that Doug have a background which would help him fulfill his deep desire to serve the Lord as an officer.

My life had been very focused on Salvation Army programming. Our three children, junior soldiers, were involved in all the activities. My experience as lay leader of various youth programs led me to respond to a question on my candidate application, "Officer-ship will be a continuation of the ministry God has already called me to: bringing God's love and his message of salvation to children and their parents."

We were able to work as a team during our years together and were blessed beyond measure! We continually learned as God led us onward. A lifetime of growing in his grace and knowledge would be difficult to condense, but the following offers a bit of wisdom from our precious privilege.

Five Wise Words of Counsel

1 Living in the neighborhood where we serve can be a blessing.

It eliminates commuting time, offers mentoring opportunities and offers a comfortable place for small group meetings which promotes freer communication. The flock we pastor can observe first-hand the Christian lifestyle in the home as well as in the community.

In our first appointment, the Army property occupied an entire circle and included playground, ball field, quarters and the corps/community center. Before we moved into our house, a group of the neighborhood's troubled teenagers had claimed a spot near the front door of the corps as their hangout before and after school. The janitor was aggravated by their disrespect – and by the cigarette butts, soda cans, etc., that they left in the area. Doug began having friendly chats with the kids whenever he saw them in the neighborhood. Living next door to the corps gave us the opportunity to develop an ongoing relationship with the group. It wasn't long before Doug brought them into the corps building, where he created a space for them to call their own for a couple of hours every day. There were definite rules and they knew if any were broken, they would lose the privileges. A sense of pride in keeping it clean led to their holding one another responsible to take good care of the furnishings. The kids eventually began attending Sunday evening salvation meetings and were introduced to the Lord Jesus! The janitor, a faithful soldier who rarely ever missed a meeting, rejoiced along with us.

We had really wondered about the quarters being right next to the corps, but as time went by, we recognized its great blessing. We knew all the neighbors; many from the surrounding streets came to big events and attended activities. Several became members of the various Salvation Army groups.

2 God wants our children to have a view of God and The Salvation Army that is positive so that they will love him with all their hearts, and feel that the Army provides wonderful opportunities to express their faith in him.

I was not prepared for balancing family, corps and community responsibility. We arrived in July, and on Christmas Eve everything was done just as had been planned for the corps and community, but … Christmas dinner at home for our little family? We went to a Chinese restaurant! Happily, it turned out to be a lovely place with white linen tablecloths and great food.

Neither had I been prepared emotionally earlier in the fall to overhear my children having a discussion about a problem they were having. One of them suggested they should talk to Mom about it … another then remarked, "Oh, Mom wouldn't have time … she's too busy with the kids at the corps."

God helped me that day to see family things needed to be as carefully planned and scheduled on the calendar as the corps and community activities.

We made having the evening meal at home together a priority. In the teenage years, because of distance to the corps, increased homework and divisional youth music activities, we allowed the children to choose whether to continue participation in the Guard and Scouting programs. We also encouraged their involvement in school activities that interested them. Today all three love the Lord and are actively engaged in the Army ranks.

3 Respecting, appreciating and joyfully following Salvation Army leadership at every level results in more effectively bringing God's love to multitudes of people.

Other officers, soldiers, employees and volunteers will observe your good spirit in following through on all that your leaders expect, and they will be more likely to do the same.

We were so blessed to have divisional leaders who not only were supportive but taught us things that would not necessarily be learned from the training curriculum. Although my husband had extensive business background, he needed instruction to properly handle the Army's unique finance systems. The financial secretary traveled to that first appointment, and we were so grateful (We had been sent out as cadet lieutenants with only the first year of training completed).

If in doubt about your leaders' reasons for a communication, speak to them personally. When the roles are reversed, remember to meet with people in dealing with issues. Carefully read letters you are about to send, keeping in mind how they will sound to the receiver. If you are uncertain, put the letter aside for a day or two, then reread for consideration. An officer sent a letter marked Personal/Confidential which my husband felt was written in haste and could have affected the young man negatively in the future. Doug sent it back to him so the officer could reconsider whether or not he really wanted to send it. After a couple of days went by, the young officer decided to tear it up. Today that young man (older and wiser now) is a very responsible dedicated officer, bringing to everyone he meets God's message of Jesus' forgiveness and the Holy Spirit's power to transform lives.

4 Knowing the people where God places us, meeting them where they are and appreciating the culture in which they are comfortable opens hearts to hear God's message of love and forgiveness.

People become accustomed to doing things a certain way. But our own comfortable ways of living, working and worshiping may not be the preferred way for those we want to reach. It's important to fit into the culture, enjoy the music and the food, recognize what is meaningful to each one and not change the style of worship nor the music that is natural in their setting.

A meeting with all who might be affected by doing something that is a bit different usually results in meaningful input. If everyone is heard and then the agreed-upon changes are implemented soon afterward, they are more likely to develop with positive acceptance.

Visiting people in their home is one way to show you care about them, and it is invaluable in building relationships with them, but some may prefer having conversation in one of the corps rooms. Some may need privacy and others need friends or family present in order to alleviate anxious feelings. Building trust that information privately shared will be kept in confidence takes time. Carefully chosen Scripture and prayer bring everyone close together as God speaks to hearts and touches deep areas of need with healing and strength.

5 Recognizing total dependence on God with whom "all things are possible" brings a trust free of doubt and fear which compels our continued obedience to the charge we committed to keep upon our commissioning.

When my husband was diagnosed with terminal cancer and then promoted to Glory one week after his 55th birthday I realized how very much I depended on him, not only for all his skills, but for my sense of security.

Perhaps it was because of the way many of us girls born before the Second World War were raised that we tended to depend on the man in our lives, and in my case, my husband was a most dependable, competent, man of wisdom and sound judgment. It had not been difficult at all to submit to his leadership, because of his loving respect and encouragement of my abilities, and his tender care and concern for me. When the "women's liberation movement" became so powerful in the 1970s, it seemed to women like me that the biblical plan which had been a blessing to us was about to be undermined. Even Salvation Army officer wives began to declare negative feelings in regard to being addressed as "Mrs. (husband's rank and name.)" There has now been full recognition of married women not only in the way they are addressed by their own rank, but in that their appointments need not be determined by their husband's. Even as some of these feelings were being verbalized and before any changes were actually in process, my husband was promoted to Glory.

I can still hear his words of encouragement before he left my side to be with the Lord: "You are going to make it ... you have such great faith in God ... you're going to be O.K!" Doug had written out every detail for me of things that had to be done, and even how to do them, such as submitting quarterly IRS business. I learned that he had even inquired of Salvation Army leadership what they might have in mind for me, and asked that they encourage me to fulfill my calling in the Army ranks.

I was very frightened about everything, not only an appointment. Each night as I thanked God for the blessings of all the experiences shared with Doug, I also began to thank God for every detail that he was now working out in my life. My realization of total dependence on God alone, and the mighty evidences of his going before me, taking care of every detail, not only restored my sense of security but also enabled me to continue carrying out my responsibilities with great joy as an officer in The Salvation Army.

Lt. Colonel Claralyn Lowman and her husband, H. Douglas Lowman, were commissioned as officers in The Salvation Army USA Eastern Territory with the Undaunted session in 1970. They served together in corps, on officer training staff, and in divisional leadership appointments until his promotion to Glory in 1992. Claralyn was then appointed to the Personnel Department at the College for Officer Training with varying responsibilities over the next 10 years, the last as director of personnel. She retired from active service in 2003 and now lives in Wilmington, Delaware.

Letter to Ephraim

By David Hammond

I am writing a personal letter to Ephraim, my dear friend and fellow worker, something like Paul wrote to his son, Timothy, centuries ago. I want to say a word of encouragement to you as you set sail on the high seas of officership in The Salvation Army. I have just passed my 80th birthday, so you understand I have more to say than can be written in one letter – 43 years as an active officer and 16 as a retired officer.

This is not about personal boasting. I do not believe in self-proclamation. Believe me, I do not want to talk about myself – only what Christ has done for me and through me, and what, by the grace of God, he is able to do through you.

Looking back

As I look back over eight decades, Ephraim, I am overflowing with thanksgiving for every appointment I have had and every person who has contributed to making me the person I am. My life has been held fast in the hands of God. As General Arnold Brown wrote on his retirement: "My life is like Laden caravans of privilege." I like what David Livingstone wrote, after traveling through Africa for a lifetime of sacrificial service: "Speak not to me of sacrifice; speak to me only of privilege."

Let me tell you of five great privileges God has bestowed upon my pilgrimage.

1 The privilege of being born into a good family

From a human point of view, there was little that was special about my family. They were of all people quite ordinary. Most people said my parents were good people. It was the kind of goodness that shone out in everything they did and in every situation of life. There was a kind of transparency that was winsome.

Remembering my father and mother, it seems that the sum of their goodness far outweighed any worldly possessions they missed. My father was hard-working, compassionate, honest and loving. My mother was nurturing, natural (she did not know what it was to put on "airs") and artistic. She loved to play the concertina on the street corner and in the hospitals. My parents were passionate about two things: first, the Army, and secondly, about dedicating their children to God for service.

I owe everything I am and have to my good parents. Their influence hovers over me every day and makes me feel that of all men, I am rich in the things that really matter. I have two sisters and one brother – all of whom surrounded me with life abundantly.

2 The privilege of knowing God's call to be an officer

I heard the call to be an officer when I was 12 years old. A visiting officer looked at me in a crowded room in our home one Sunday night and planted words I never forgot: "David, I think that someday you are going to become a Salvation Army officer." For nine years, I kept the secret to myself and never told a soul as these words repetitiously rang in my ears like a broken record.

When I was 20, one month from my 21st birthday, I knew it was decision time. I had to make up my mind and choose between the broad way (that leads to destruction) and the narrow way (which leads to life). In a youth meeting, January 28, 1951, at about 8:30 p.m. I stood up from where I was sitting in the trombone section of a small band and made my way to the Mercy Seat – a practice that was rare in my experience. When I knelt at a very plain chair, a kind lady came and put her arms around and said, "Is there something I can do to help you, David?"

I replied, "I think something has already happened to me." Halfway between my place in the band and the Mercy Seat, I felt the hand of God accepting the sacrifice of my life to be a servant of Jesus Christ as an officer. It was a defining moment that changed the course of my life and opened the door to more than 60 years of covenant service under the flag of The Salvation Army.

It would be impossible to tell you how much spiritual fruit has come into my life through 60 years of officership. I do not think a large book could capture everything God has done through me. When I was 20, I thought long and hard about committing my whole life to an unknown path, controlled by an unknown authority, leaping into an unknown future. Now that I am over 80, in the light of what I have come to understand what Jesus has done for me, it seems, as Paul writes to the Romans "Only the reasonable thing to do."

I feel that if I had taken the opportunity of writing my own life course, I could not have done it better. I learned to trust God and let things work out for good – and they did. I never once asked for an appointment, nor refused to go where the Army sent me.

3 The privilege of a magnificent life partner

After 53 years with my life partner, unexpectedly and without warning, she went home to be with Jesus. I owe her a debt I cannot repay. She loved me with an unconditional compassion, as she did everyone around her. She was a role model par excellence.

Ephraim: I write this only to point out the importance of choosing well your life partner. Take time to pray about it with patience and obedience and God will give you the right person at the right time. To be unequally yoked with an unsuitable partner will severely handicap your ministry. God has someone good for you, believe me.

4 The privilege of children and grandchildren

After a bumpy start, the Lord gave us two children, along with their spouses. In addition, we have eight grandchildren. They are an unending source of joy and delight in a thousand ways, which only grandparents can comprehend.

But with the gift of new life comes sacred responsibility to raise children in the nurture and admonition of the Lord. Never underestimate the subtle power of world influences which come to our children in a thousand ways, many beyond our control. Nurturing and training our children in the way of the Lord demands close attention, careful guidance and prayerful supervision. It will take the cooperative efforts of both parents, using patience and compassion.

5 The privilege of serving in the Army

Above all, I feel of all people most privileged to have served my whole life in the Army. If life could be lived all over again, I would sign up without hesitation, except, I would hope to serve better, with more zeal, more compassion and more fidelity.

The Salvation Army has its weakness and failings, as any organization does, but then we know that not one of us can claim to be perfect. I believe the Army is part of the body of Christ, and when we kick and destructively criticize the Army, we injure the very body of Christ. Jesus feels the pain for misdirected, loveless words.

Looking forward

I want to turn my eye in a forward direction and think about you and your future in the Army, Ephraim. What can I say that will encourage you, prepare you, strengthen you for the ministry?

1 Prayer is pivotal

The best advice I can give you is to make prayer the heart and soul of everything you do every day, every year, every decade. It may be that this is where the devil will seek to deflect your attention and lead you into a prayerless life.

You do not need anything more than the example of Jesus. His life, from the very beginning, was saturated in prayer. Mary and Joseph worshiped regularly at the synagogue and saw that Jesus was steeped in the Hebrew faith. Jesus made a habit of spending whole nights in prayer, often after long and draining days of teaching and preaching. He prayed in every critical moment of his short years of ministry; in the Garden of Gethsemane he prayed, "Father, if it be possible, let this cup pass from me;" and he prayed to his Father during his six hours on the cross, words that Christians for centuries have been exploring.

Jesus spent much of his time teaching his disciples to pray. Without prayer, our lives will be fruitless for the Kingdom.

Find time to enter your closet, closing the door and praying to your Father. He promises to reward us richly beyond our expectations and our imagination. Make your prayer life the most important activity of your daily schedule.

2 Time is precious

The most precious possession any officer has is time. Time is a priceless gift that does not last forever. It moves imperceptibly from birth to death, and no power on earth can stop it. Looking ahead, time may seem like an eternity; but looking back, it moves faster than a weaver's shuttle – quicker than the twinkling of the eye. Make the most of the time you have. Do not waste it or think carelessly of it. Take Tennyson's advice: "Fill the unforgiving minute with sixty seconds worth of distance run."

Learn to discipline your time every day. That does not mean that you have no time to relax and smell the roses, or to pursue your golf game. Organize and prioritize your time so that you put the first things first. Remember that someday you will have to stand before your Master and give an account of how you have invested your time.

3 The Bible is priceless

I read of a survey taken among ministers, indicating that 85 percent of clergy had no devotional life. I hope it does not apply to Salvation Army officers. I hope it will not apply to you. Don't become too busy to pray, too busy to read the Bible and think deeply about the gospel message. Many ministers are dabblers in many things, but every minister of the gospel should be a master of one thing: the Bible.

Dietrich Bonhoeffer, the courageous German clergyman who spoke out against Hitler's Nazi regime, wrote: "Every day for me is lost that I have not penetrated deeper into the understanding of God in Scripture."

Think of it carefully,
Study it prayerfully,

Deep in thy heart,
Let its oracles dwell.
Ponder its mysteries,
Slight not its histories,
None can love it too fondly or well.

4 Ministry is personal

In studying the ministry of Jesus, one learns that ministry is always personal. It was individuals like Nicodemus, the unnamed woman at the well, Zacheaus, Peter, James and John. Who captured Jesus' eye? The lost, the lonely and the least. Follow the example of your leader – go and do likewise.

It does not mean that crowds are unimportant, but crowds are made up of individuals. Crowds are of value only so long as one thinks that every crowd is a compilation of individuals.

The good shepherd who, when counting his flock, found one absent, left the 90 and nine and went out looking one lost sheep. What a lesson he taught us. Every person counts; every person has a name. Jesus died for every lost soul.

5 Our destiny is promised

Finally, keep your eyes on the prize. Look beyond this present world of time and space and material things. Look to Jesus and his Kingdom – *the new Jerusalem, coming down out of heaven from*

God (Revelation 21:2). From the cross Jesus gave the dying thief the greatest promise of all – "*Today you shall be with me in paradise*" (Luke 23:43). It is a promise he also gives to us. Jesus said: "*I go to prepare a place for you so that where I am you may be also*" *(John 14:3)*. It is one of greatest and surest promises of the Bible.

My witness to you, Ephraim:

I feel that the last drops of my life are being poured out for God. The glorious fight that God gave me I have fought, the course I set I have finished, and I have kept the faith. The future holds for me a crown of righteousness which God, the righteous judge, will give me in that day (2 Timothy 4:6-8).

My charge to you:

I charge you to live in the sight of God and of Christ Jesus ... to preach the word of God. Never lose your sense of urgency, in and out of season. Prove, correct and encourage, using the utmost of patience in your teaching. Go on steadily preaching the gospel and carry out the full commission that God gave you (2 Timothy 4: 1-5 J.B. Phillips).

God bless you, my friend, Ephraim. As often as I think of you, I will pray for you.

Lt. Colonel David Hammond is the son of the late Major David and Rhoda Hammond and was born in Winnipeg, Manitoba. He was a member of the Intercessors session (1951-52) and has served as an active and retired officer for 64 years. His last three appointments were five years as training college principal in St John's, Newfoundland, five years as divisional commander in the Maritime Division and five years as editor-in-chief of publications in the Canadian-Bermuda Territory. He has always been passionate about communicating through the printed word and lifting high the triune God – Father, Son, and Holy Spirit – through the Army.

Foundations

By Todd Bassett

It seems almost presumptuous for someone who is 40 years removed from his last field appointment to be giving words of council to those just entering their first command. However, I share the following primarily from the perspective of 13 years of divisional leadership.

These thoughts are based on the fundamental belief that there is nothing more important than a quality prayer life and the continuous study of God's Word. *Seek first the Kingdom of God and his righteousness* (Matthew 6:33).

As I look back, the five words that I suggest that can be foundational as you face forward toward your officership are: love, honor, purpose, passion and humility.

Love

It is easy to mouth the words spoken by Jesus that the greatest commandment is wrapped up in our love for the Lord and our love for others. But some people as well as some appointments are not easy to love. Learn to love! Your love for life, love for your people, love for your leaders, love for who you are in Christ and the work that he has called you to do are essential. Believe in yourself and believe that the Lord will give you the capacity to love in each of these areas. *Love from the center of who you are; don't fake it. Run for dear life from evil; hold on for dear life to good. Be good friends who love deeply; practice playing second fiddle.* (Romans 12: 9,10 The Message)

Honor

Self-will is one of the greatest challenges in the life of a Christian, regardless of the calling. The willingness to be submissive to the Lord and those that he has allowed to be placed over you as a result of your calling will not always be easy. This is especially true if you are a free thinker. This is not an urging for you to be an "institutional thinker," but to be a person who respects and honors those over you. You will always want to conduct yourself in an honorable fashion. Honor yourself as you honor others. *Submit yourself for the Lord's sake to every human institution ... for such is the will of God that by doing right you may silence the ignorance of the foolish man* (1 Peter 2:13, 14 NAS).

Passion

Give it all you've got! Don't hold back and wait for a more convenient opportunity. Whether it is preaching the Word, collecting for Christmas, doing the janitorial work or the most demeaning task required, do it like Christ would do it! People will be watching to see if you are genuine. Zeal and enthusiasm are contagious and will abound in your corps or institution if you show that you are really committed to your calling. You will attract others to follow you and the Lord! Be positive in how you lead your people. *Looking for the blessed hope and the appearing of the glory of our great God and Savior, Christ Jesus, who gave Himself for us to redeem us from every lawless deed, and to purify for Himself a people for His own possession, zealous for good deeds.* (Titus 2:13, 14 NASB)

Purpose

Understand what your management and leadership styles are. Then get yourself organized. Establish clear priorities and direction for your life and ministry. The Lord has you where you are for a purpose and you are responsible to discover it and make sure you fulfill God's purpose. There are consequences for every action and there will be times when you will fail. But that hardly matters as much as how you handle the failure and if you learn by that situation. We are not perfect and the Lord certainly understands that; and he even extends his grace and forgiveness to us. *Live life, then, with a due sense of responsibility, not as men who do not know the meaning and purpose of life but as those who do. … firmly grasp what you know to be the will of the Lord.* (Ephesians 5: 15-17 J.B. Phillips)

Humility

Let no man think more highly of himself than he ought. We are to do justly, love mercy and walk humbly with the Lord. It is certainly possible to be confident and yet be humble, realizing that what we are able to do and who we are is a gift from the Lord. We are entrusted with the awesome task of being personal representatives of our Lord Jesus Christ. In this work we work together with God. It is he who calls and equips and we are never to become proud of the places he will take us or the wisdom that may flow from our lips. Our uniform and the name The Salvation Army will open doors and opportunities you never dreamed of, and you are to be Christ's ambassador! *And so, as those who have been chosen of God, holy and beloved, put on a heart of compassion, kindness, humility, gentleness and patience* (Colossians 3:12 NIV).

Looking back, I can see in each of these areas where I have succeeded as well as how I failed. However, I know that throughout the 42 years of active officership and in the four years of active retirement, the Lord has never failed to provide and sustain me as his servant. It is great to be a Salvation Army officer!

May the Holy One be your guide and strength as you look forward to the coming days of ministry and service.

Commissioner W. Todd Bassett retired in 2006 having served as the USA National Commander. Todd is a graduate of Asbury University. As an active officer he has had appointments in the areas of corps officer, youth ministry, training and territorial and International Headquarters. Following retirement, he served as the executive director of the National Evangelical Association. Todd presently finds fulfillment serving as the pastoral care leader, teaching an adult Bible class, and serving as a bandsman and songster at the Old Orchard Beach, Maine, Corps.

A Conversation About Salvation Army Officership

General Paul A. Rader and Commissioner Kay F. Rader

What follows is a conversation between General Paul A. Rader and Commissioner Kay F. Rader reflecting on their calling and experience as officers of The Salvation Army.

PAR: A lifetime of service certainly gives us a unique perspective on officership over the long haul.

KFR: Long, but never boring. How often have we said, we may die of something, but it won't be of boredom!

PAR: Is there any calling that is more diverse, colorful, fascinating, challenging and rewarding than officership? Not a walk in the park – sometimes intense and demanding, but always deeply rewarding.

KFR: What do you think has kept us at it all these years?

PAR: Bottom line: a sense of calling. The confidence that this is God's will for our lives. We have to admit that how that call is experienced is not the same for everyone.

KFR: Isaiah 30:21 tells us, *Your ears will hear a word behind you, 'This is the way, walk in it.*" I wish it could be that certain for everyone.

PAR: Psalm 32:8 has always been reassuring for me: *I will instruct you and teach you in the way you should go; I will counsel you with my loving eye on you.* God has a way of opening a door and nudging us toward it by his Spirit.

KFR: Yes! Those who have ears to hear and hearts to obey want to respond as Isaiah did when he was touched with fire, "Here am I, send me!" However it comes, a settled sense that we are on the path of God's purpose as officers has taken us through the difficult points in the journey.

PAR: And there have been some testing times.

KFR: For one thing, we never knew where our response to God's call was going to take us. I love the plaque in our kitchen that pictures a little tent topped with an Army flag and says, "Home is where the Army sends me!" Along with all the positive and the Divine Yes that resonates in our hearts, we accept the disciplines of an Army – an Army of Salvation, an Army of peace, but nevertheless an Army. And that means being wherever we are needed in the line of battle.

PAR: Officership is not about contract. It is about covenant. It begins with our commitment to Jesus Christ and the reality of our relationship to him. It is grounded in our experience of his saving life. Our relationship to him is covenantal. And when we have responded to his call, our relationship to the Army is really not unlike the marriage covenant. Officers enter into a covenant relationship of trust and loyal commitment: each to the other, and both to God. The Army commits to provide for its officers as long as they are faithful to their calling. The Army depends on us and we depend on the Army. But there is no binding legal contract. It is all a matter of calling and covenant, mutual trust and commitment.

KFR: One of the great joys of officership for married couples is the privilege of working so closely together in a common calling. We have been able to work off of each other's strengths, supporting and encouraging one another. As married officers we signed individual covenants, committing us to "live to win souls … as the first great purpose of [our lives] … to be true to The Salvation Army, and the principles represented by its Flag." But the Army, after all, is about teamwork, an egalitarian partnership that crosses gender lines gently.

PAR: The covenant is not intended to be joint. It is a transaction that must occur between the individual and God. It is, however, signed and sealed with a common purpose that is shared by all officers, whether one's spouse or a colleague officer with whom we may be teamed – all of this, as an accepted part of God's plan for our lives as officers in The Salvation Army.

KFR: Our covenant committed us to the holy mission of the Army. It has been expressed in many ways. The International Mission Statement is this:

> *The Salvation Army, an international movement, is an evangelical part of the universal Christian Church. Its message is based on the Bible. Its ministries are motivated by love for God. Its mission is to preach the gospel of Jesus Christ and meet human need in his name without discrimination.*

Our calling and covenant commit us to the mission. Officership requires allegiance to the mission, under the lordship of Jesus Christ, believing in its principles and goals and methods and being fully comfortable with its ethos.

PAR: That is why full immersion in the training experience is so critical.

KFR: One of the most exciting dimensions of officership is the wide open door it provides for creativity and innovation in our service. There is such a rich diversity of ministry opportunities.

And always fresh ways to address the needs of those we serve and with whom we share the gospel.

PAR: For one thing, officership makes us part of a global missionary movement. It can provide a platform for service anywhere in the world. It puts us totally at God's disposal to send us where he will and use us as he will.

KFR: Officership does not give us a blank sheet of paper and a packet of crayons and say draw whatever you want. But within the expectations and guidelines the Army affords – and the Army itself is part of a divinely creative process – there is unlimited scope for a lifetime of ministry as colorful and inventive as God by his Spirit can help us to make it.

PAR: We need to say something about officership being long-term. It is not a sprint. It's a marathon. OK, that is a hard sell these days – maybe more than ever before. People tend to be into short-term commitments with all options open and unhampered control of one's life choices. Let's be honest. When God laid his hand hot upon us and claimed us by his grace for this ministry, it meant signing on for the duration.

KFR: Actually, the Soldier's Covenant (what we used to call The Articles of War), signed by every soldier, commits us to a lifetime covenant of service within the Army. It is part of the uniqueness of our movement that we expect that level of commitment from all our members. Officer covenants go deeper by extending this promise to exclude other employment outside the bounds of the Army until retirement, and an expectation that even after retirement, officers will give willing service as opportunities arise. This is long term.

In the early days of overseas missionary service, the candidate understood his/her covenant to be lifelong. British born Amy Carmichael, famous missionary to India, committed her life to the people of India for a lifetime, never returning home for furlough, living out her life, dying and being buried among the people of the Dohnavuhr Fellowship, which she founded. Elisabeth Elliott titled her biography of this great saint "A Chance to Die."

PAR: Officership provides its own "chance to die" and "chance to live" for heaven's highest purpose: sharing the gospel in its transforming power and living out the love of Christ for our lost and broken world. For *he died for all, that those who live should no longer live for themselves, but for him who died and was raised again* (2 Corinthians 5:14 TNIV). But let's be up front about the cost, because Jesus was. *"Whoever wants to be my disciple,"* Jesus said, *"must deny themselves and take up their cross daily and follow me. For whoever wants to save their life will lose it, but whoever loses their life for me will save it"* (Luke 9:23, 24 TNIV).

KFR: Officership is long-term service: service to God and the Army for a lifetime. Officership is not working for the Army. Officership is *being* the Army. Officership is *belonging* to an elite "company of the committed." The fellowship among the officers with whom we may be privileged to serve is beautiful.

PAR: What a privilege to wear the same uniform they wear. We have met them all over the world – many serving in hostile environments, in difficult and dangerous circumstances. The uniforms may differ but they are all identifiable as Army. When we meet these heroes and heroines, we know we share a common covenant and are engaged in the same great mission. The uniform itself is sacramental. Putting it on may be difficult, but as one Korean officer observed, "taking it off is more difficult."

KFR: Whatever the challenges, the rewards of this life are great beyond telling. And best of all is knowing that to follow Christ into officership in answer to his call is to bring joy to the heart of God. In the end, that is all that matters.

General Paul A. Rader (Ret.) is a former international leader of The Salvation Army, elected in 1994 and serving with his wife, Commissioner Kay F. Rader until their retirement in 1999; she, as World President of Salvation Army Women's Ministries. For 22 years they were missionary officers serving in Korea. From 2000 to 2006 he was president of their alma mater, Asbury University, in Wilmore, Kentucky. Their story is told in "If Two Shall Agree" by Carroll Hunt Rader. In 2015 they published "To Seize This Day of Salvation" released during the Boundless Congress. The Raders live in Lexington, Kentucky, and are avid runners.

CHARGE!

F. Joyce Kerr

We all started our officership with Commissioning events. I had forgotten the exact wording, so I had to go back and find a copy of what I had actually committed myself to in The Declaration of Faith and The Doctrines of the Salvation Army. This was then followed by our commitment to the words that we would strive to lead all persons to their only Savior and for his sake to care for the poor, feed the hungry, clothe the naked, love the unlovable and befriend those who have no friends.

We then promised that by holy living, boundless charity and adherence to the principles and disciplines of the Army to show ourselves at all times to be faithful officers of The Salvation Army. The officiating officer accepted the declarations and promises that we made on this special day.

Responsibility: obedience to the principles of the Army

Following our engagement, Don applied to be allowed to take teacher training and be sent to the Northern British Columbia Division, where there always seemed to be a shortage of teachers. As a result of the Army's approval we were married in June in Toronto and then traveled back to Vancouver. After a week of married life Don attended university and I was on the train to our first appointment in Glen Vowel, a little Army village strung along the Skeena River. There I was on my own, in a village of about 100 people with no running water, no electricity, no stores, the closest being eight miles away and no transport. Different for a city girl, but hitching a ride to town soon became a way of life – in full uniform, by the way.

Why am I telling you this? It relates to our determination and commitment to never refuse a change of appointment.

Obedience and fulfillment

In over 43 years of active service we never turned down an appointment. We had lots of questions we shared with the Lord but obediently packed up and moved on to the next challenge. There was just one occasion that was different. When we were the divisional leaders in Northern BC, Don received a phone call from the chief secretary asking him if he would accept an appointment as the assistant principal at the training college. Don was stuck for words. He asked if he could have time to contact me as I was out of the city. The chief secretary said, "Yes," but he would need an answer by the next day. Don, still stunned, asked the colonel,"What should I do?" His reply: "I would suggest you accept." We were in the smallest division and farthest away from THQ and had had no direct contact with the college since our training days.

Preaching

In retirement, I am concerned that we seem to be losing out in our preaching and teaching of the Doctrine of Holiness. Salvation is vital, but for people to grow and remain established in their walk with the Lord, there must be a realization and acceptance of the need for the life of holiness. I know in my day we had in most corps holiness meetings in the morning and salvation in the evening and a weekly meeting for soldiers' teaching. Today, most corps have only one service but we must still be committed to preach what we believe. We are a holiness movement, and we need holy people to fulfill our mission. Don't lose the vision of holiness. Remember to fulfill the promises you made at your commissioning.

Price – Yes, there is a cost to our commitment as officers

Sometimes the responsibilities overwhelm us, not enough hours in the day, and sometimes our family feels the stress of

Mom's busyness. During a visit of the DYS to our corps, he had a conversation with our third child. He also took a picture of her and it ended up on the front cover of *The Young Soldier* for Mother's Day, with the quote – "My mother works for the Salvation Army – my mother is never home!"

It brought me up short, and that evening I had to find some personal time to chat with her. We talked about when I was home: saw her off to school, home at lunch time, home after school, tucked her into bed before going out to the corps. Well, yes, she agreed, but you seem to be always in a rush, not really here. It was a busy time for me, and she was right – my mind was working overtime, and she felt neglected. The Lord and I had some long chats and he gave me the wisdom to tune into the children and put my workload on hold. We have four children and felt that one of us must always be available as needed, and so a lot of my workload could be done from home. The nights I was out, Don was home. We tried to limit our babysitters to Sunday nights and one other night when necessary. That worked for many years, but every once in a while I had to remind myself the children were God's gift and he made me aware of the commitment I had as a parent. It's harder to connect when the children are in their teens and involved in outside commitments and all of us going in different directions – but it is our responsibility to have a schedule that keeps us in touch as a family.

I am now in my 18th year of retirement; adding the active years makes 61 years of officership. When I started out as a cadet, I had no idea of the future and what it would bring to me. During those days at the training college, the Lord gave me a special Scripture portion to take with me for a lifetime. Don't get me wrong – he gave me other portions and words of advice for specific situations. But these particular words have stayed with me so that from the least questions to the big problems, to the times of joy and celebration, these words would calm my spirit and allow me to trust him for his guidance. Just whisper them, and he will be there for you.

Trust in the Lord with all your heart and lean not on your own understanding; in all your ways acknowledge him and he will make your paths straight (Proverbs 3:5-6).

The daughter of Colonels Knaap, Commissioner Joyce Kerr came out of the old Mt. Dennis Corps in Canada, commissioned in 1955. She and her husband, Don, raised three daughters and one son. A gifted speaker through various appointments in corps, training and at headquarters in England and Canada, she ended her active service as the president for women's organizations of the Canada and Bermuda Territory. Upon retirement she also led a popular weekly Bible study for many years.

A Gentrified Joe! (Part 2)

By Joe Noland

Those were the days my friend
We thought they'd never end.

Ever analyzed why those street corner open-air days ended? Here is the excuse I've heard most often, personally even uttering it myself on occasion.

"Those were the days when street corners were community gathering places, but that has all changed with the advent of television, mega-malls and the internet. People no longer gather on those corners as they once did."

Translation: "That was scary stuff and sometimes embarrassing, especially with our newfound acceptance and brand image. Let's get in step with the 21st century emerging 'sophisticated' us!"

Last evening, Doris and I took a stroll down Kalakaua Avenue, in Waikiki, past the International Marketplace. Lo and behold, there were street performers of every stripe entertaining hundreds of bystanders: musicians, artists, clowns, balloon shapers, a gold-plated human statue, foot massagers and even Elmo, each with a "collection device" (no tambourines apparent), all drawing crowds. Standing there for a few minutes watching Elmo do his thing, I calculated that his collecting device was filling at the pace of several dollars per minute ($120/hour), not a bad day's work, huh? And, besides, he was brightening the evening for a lot of people.

We've witnessed this phenomenon wherever we've been lately: Melbourne, Sydney, Brisbane, London, Times Square, NYC (The Naked Cowboy?), Boston, Dallas, Denver, Hollywood and, yes, Fisherman's Wharf, San Francisco (a man behind a portable bush jumped out and scared us silly, while bystanders laughed and happily contributed to his retirement fund). But alas! The Salvation Army isn't there anymore "because people no longer gather on the street corners."

Another modern phenomenon (perhaps related) is the gentrification of cities, far and wide. We were recently in Old Town Pasadena, the streets bustling with hordes of people, seemingly going nowhere. And the historic Gas Lamp Quarter in San Diego, where they now conduct ghost tours in what was once an old haunt of mine. I wonder if the ghosts of Horton Plaza open-airs past are on their itinerary? It's amazing to see the transformation occurring – keeping the ambience of the past, yet simultaneously conforming to the culture of a new day.

Gentrification: the process of transforming… into something more prosperous.

Standing on that transformed Market, Powell and Eddy Mall in San Francisco (See Part 1), I reflect upon the ghosts of open-airs past. Moments of doubt cloud my thinking. Was the demise of street-corner meetings related to changing demographics, or is it because The Salvation Army was transforming into something more prosperous, gentrifying, if you will?

Hasn't Peter Drucker tabbed us, "The most effective organization in the U.S.?" *Reader's Digest* wrote, "The charity you can trust." *Forbes magazine* reported, "One of the top 10 charities that shine … one that gives supporters more bang for their buck." *The Chronicle of Philanthropy* stated, "America's favorite and most trusted charity." How would Joe the Turk fare in today's gentrified Army culture, I wonder?

Gentrification isn't bad, mind you; it's a good thing, so long as we adapt evangelistically to an ever-changing culture.

Where to from here, backward or forward? Perhaps a mixture of both, huh? *Those were the days my friend, They need not ever end*, with a little gentrification thrown in for good measure, of course. Or as that *haunting* voice from the past keeps reminding us, "Adaptation is our only law!" (Catherine Booth)

These are the days my friend
Adaptation never ends
We'll sing and dance
Forever and a day
We'll live the life we choose
We'll fight and never lose
Yes, forever young
And sure to have his way
La La La, etc.

Given a second chance to redeem the past 50-something years, I would also consider the following three things prayerfully:

1 *Examine* (my) *excuses* carefully. Are they motivated by fear and a desire for comfort, or are they based in reality?

2 *Embrace change* fully. There is something about "We've always done it this way!" that is familiar, comforting and soothing. And if I'm going to continue doing it "this way," my excuses are (were) valid and legitimate.

3 *Enforce* (the law of) *adaptability* always. The modern word for it is *gentrification*, keeping the core values (infrastructure) intact, while ever melding them, progressively, into a transforming culture.

I confess to making many excuses, resisting or ignoring change too often and hanging on dearly to those comforting, traditional things that helped shape me as a person and Salvationist. Looking back, here is my combined charge to future leaders who are now facing forward:

1-Fight fearlessly!

2-Get a (faith) grip!

3-Examine (all) excuses!

4-Embrace change!

5-Enforce (the law of) adaptability!

Oh, and by the way, Joe the Turk would draw enormous crowds today at the transformed San Francisco Market, Powell and Eddy Plaza. A gentrified Joe, of course!

And what if it were all captured on video and spread through social media? Just think!

Epilogue

By Stephen Court

Those of us involved in The Salvation Army know something of tyranny of the urgent. We are inundated with interruptions. We are disturbed and our schedules disrupted by demands on our time. Now, in our reflective moments we realize that often the interruptions are divine in origin and the demands are from God. But sometimes they are not …

We know something of duty. Many of us have imbibed of grace by the pathway of duty and too often in the weekly grind of corps schedule we forget that God's river of grace still flows there.

We know something of distraction. Was it easier in the old days when there was no internet, no iPhones (or any mobile devices, for that matter), no DVDs, no cable TV, no, no, no …? Maybe it was simpler. But we are flooded with distractions from the world pressuring us to conform to standards of comfort that are inharmonious with the demands of the salvation war. We have proven that it is far easier to settle than to attack.

We know something of ecumenical influence. We may not know Brengle and Booth like the writers of this volume do, but we seem to know Saddleback and Willow Creek and Jakes and Hillsong well enough. And conferences, podcasts, blogs, CDs, books, TV and other media swamp us with non-Salvo theology and non-Salvo mission, deadening our spirits to the aggressive salvation war to which we have covenanted our lives.

All of these things we know can often compete to potentially drag us from optimal impact for the Kingdom of God.

And here we have gathered 600 years of active officership. The advice from these veterans comes from a better vantage point than we enjoy. Higher up the mountain, these experienced leaders have a better perspective on the race.

What are they telling us? For many readers their lessons are more reminders than new revelation. But here is an alphabet's summary of some of their advice, in the categories – Inward, Upward, Outward:

Inward

a. Keep daily with your rations, your personal, private time with God. Time is precious. We have to be ruthless on this one, keeping daily on our time with God for prayer and

Bible. Every sin, every moral failure, every breach of covenant, every descent into mediocrity, every case of settling with coasting to retirement started with a break in the streak.

b. Sort out your stuff first. There is an apostolic principle Peter exemplifies with the beggar when he confesses that he has no money but then goes ahead and heals the man. It is this: You cannot give what you do not have. At one corps where I soldiered, "issues" was slang in mixed company for demons. "She's got issues" meant that she had demons that we needed to confront. Confront your demons – and I mean that literally – now, so that you can confront others' demons from a position of purity and authority.

c. Keep accountable to someone. This is easy to slide by. Not only be accountable, but be formally accountable, not casually accountable, as in "I get together with the boys once a month and we keep each other on track." This can happen in discipling relationships or mutual accountability groups, Wesley's class meetings, soldiers meetings or other inventions. Infinitum is a rule of life Salvationists have started that provides an excellent context for accountability and discipleship (infinitumlife.com). But lack of accountability gives demons the day off.

d. Keep the joy of the Lord. Our writers generously assume we enjoy the joy of the Lord now. Tragically, some of us don't. Salvationists, historically, are characterized by it. One could go so far as to suggest that without the joy you aren't a Salvo. Joy is deeper than duty. And fulfillment of covenant by duty instead of joy is like dragging a train across a desert instead of along the train tracks.

e. Keep humble and joyfully give glory to God. None of us is Jesus. None of us is even William Booth. Anything we contribute will be at most a branch of Booth's tree. So let's keep some perspective. And the Army has lost many more gifted leaders to sin and greener pastures than most of us are – and it keeps on expanding (praise God). All of that to say we aren't 'all of that' and the Army doesn't even really need us. Our only true success is in our spiritual death, in which case humility is part of the deal.

f. Conviction of calling. Regardless of whether it came in a three-hour glory fit or the realization of the need, know you are doing what God wants you to be doing. Covenant is serious business. And God keeps covenants (even if you made it wrongly). Does God want you to be a plumber or a teacher or a chimney sweep? Great! Do it with all of your might. But if he hasn't clarified for you his vocational purposes, then train up for officership. As Bramwell Booth wrote: "The great need of the world – its lost condition – is sufficient call for anyone who has the opportunity to respond." Conviction of calling will get you through all kinds of battles and temptations. And a covenant of conviction will get you through the rest.

g. Don't compromise. There are all kinds of pressures to compromise. The difficulty of the salvation war on the local front tempts compromise. Though we covenant to live to win souls and make their salvation the primary purpose of our lives, in some places, in some seasons, it seems like not too many people get saved. And that makes it hard to sleep at night. When you can't sleep because of paucity of converts and disciples, it is easier to be able to rationalize that we fed 25 people and clothed 19 people and housed six. And that is the start of strategic compromise. Spiritual compromise looks like personal rations (prayer/Bible) morphing into preaching preparation until you rationalize that your Bible study preparation and preaching preparation "counts" for your own personal development. And there are all kinds of similar compromises.

Upward

h. Read books. Amen. Can I suggest that you read Salvation Army books, and books by dead people? If half of your titles are Salvo and half by dead people, you will do well to avoid too much non-Salvo influence and too much trendy thought that has not stood the test of time.

i. Be incarnational. Live where you fight and fight where you live. It is biblical. And it is effective. It may be a bit of a hassle to move a quarters. It may require more difficult living conditions and more basic schooling and so on. But that is where Jesus is.

j. Continue to get better equipped. You want to be a more effective warrior and leader in 20 years than you are now. How do you get there? Prepare. It may involve getting a mentor, or reading some books, or putting yourself into challenging situations (like mission trips or Booth-Tucker Institute or special projects), or attending a conference, or taking a course. It will involve extraordinary prayer.

k. Be an encourager. If you are early in your leadership, you remember well what it is to participate out of love. Keep remembering that all of your people, your soldiers, your local officers, your converts and recruits are all there because they want to be. They don't have to be. They exercise exemplary commitment to a cause in which they believe. They don't get paid. They don't, in western cultures, get any social benefit from belonging. Ensure that they are encouraged in the fight.

l. Stay the course. These writers have all stayed the course.

They know what it is to fight with integrity in season and out, during times of favor and times of attack, with much and with little. They have proven their character. They have proven faithful. A crown of righteousness awaits them. Hallelujah. But not only them – it also awaits each of us who longs for his appearing. Keep longing for the Lord's appearing and you will stay the course.

m. Love God and love your neighbor. This is the whole shooting match in a nutshell, to mangle cliches! This is holiness on a thumbnail. This is the sum and substance of God's expectation and provision. God is good, and what God commands, God enables. He commands holiness manifest as perfect love, and praise God that he provides for it. Don't settle for anything less. It is not uncommon to find those who like God and put up with their neighbors. But let's fully obey God ...

n. Remember the privilege. Tragically, The Salvation Army has a bit of a problem with the sense of entitlement. Partly because the Army has been so paternalistic and caring in providing for corps and officers, corps and soldiers and officers have grown complacent. Many of us assume that we are entitled to what God blesses us with in the Army. We are not entitled. It is a privilege for each of us to have covenanted with God through the Army as soldiers and, some of us, as officers. God, help us remember it, please.

o. Purpose. We're here to help win the world for Jesus. We're not here to "coddle the saints" (Cadman). We're not satisfied with growing our corps or enrolling soldiers or sending candidates into officership. The world is lost, and Jesus is coming to take it back. And we're meant to fight alongside him, rescuing as many as we can from sin and hell. Don't be distracted from this purpose or settle for anything less or anything else.

p. Honor. Don't just submit to your leaders, but honor them. There is room for a great distinction here. Attitude is crucial here. And the distinction extends from attitude with the Lord. We can obey the Lord with a poor attitude. And that does not honor him. It is the same with the divisional commander, the territorial commander and the General. And it is the same for the retired Home League member, the lifelong bandsman and the welcome sergeant.

Outward

q. Fight fearlessly. We need to put on the full armor of God and take our stand against the rulers, authorities and principalities that threaten us and our people at every turn. We need to remember that we are sent to a district and that most of the people in that district are living in rebellion against God. We need to, "fight, live to fight, love to fight, love the thickest of the fight, and die in the midst of it" (William Booth). Salvos love to fight and fight with love.

r. Enjoy your work. This should not be difficult. After all, we each offered for it. And there is a significant amount of autonomy included so that you are free to focus on what you understand God to be emphasizing on your local front. You are investing in the lives of people and replicating yourself in them. You live a concentrated lifestyle that ideally is either taking it in or giving it out. There is so much to enjoy.

s. Practice servanthood. There is always a tension here. You don't want to be the only person doing all the work in the corps because it is not spiritually healthy for the corps officer to be the one who picks up all the old folks for the meeting and shovels the driveway and hands out the bulletins. But you don't want to be so far removed from the coalface that you miss out on the life of the people. The fellowship is in the fight. To truly know your people, you need to fight alongside them, and that includes the most humble of service. Jesus sets the example. Brengle's boot-shining sets a standard for leaders.

t. Preach for a verdict. The Salvation Army is an ultra-revivalist movement, according to one encyclopedia. That means we aim for immediate results. The climax of every Salvation Army meeting is meant to be the prayer meeting – the appeal following the preaching. Transaction with God and its concomitant transformation is what we are all about. To miss out on that or to go light on it is to betray the covenantal trust God has in us. Go hard.

u. Positively engage with all people in your community (Christians AND others). You are sent to a district. Get involved in the district. There are all kinds of people there – Muslims, Hindus, Sikhs, Hell's Angels, atheists and just plain sinners. Don't be offended by some of their more overt sins. Sinners sin – that's what they do. And, remember, Jesus died for each of them. We were all like them before we received the mercy of our great God and Savior, Jesus Christ. As community members engage in community projects and justice initiatives, they will have opportunity to see your Holy Spirit-character and be attracted to Jesus in you.

v. "I am convinced there is just no more time for small talk, petty differences, greed, power struggles and jockeying for positions of so-called authority." This one is from a commissioner. It is a helpful perspective. Time is short. People are dying and going to hell. Let's do all that is possible to save them. So let's not just aim to add a soldier here and there. Let's aim to multiply bases (base = cells + infinitum hubs) and outposts and corps. Let's aim to invade apartment complexes and cities and countries. Let's aim to win the world for Jesus.

w. Embrace change. You nod your head in eager agreement now. Let's see how you respond in 20 years when you re-read it. This is not change for the sake of change. It is change for the sake of optimizing our effectiveness in the salvation war. Don't throw babies out with bath water. And make sure that you aren't changing things to make your schedule lighter or easier. But some changes will enable you to impact more people with the gospel. Adaptability is a basic principle elucidated by Catherine Booth. It was modeled by William Booth in his automobile evangelism, by Herbert Booth in film innovation, by Arnold Brown in television, and so on. Embrace it.

x. Understand the world. We are meant to know what our neighbors' lives are like. What scares them? What entertains them? What tempts them? What distresses them? Answers to these questions inform our war-fighting. But we will benefit also from knowing something of the larger trends of humanity in politics and economics and religion and culture. This is part of the incarnational mandate.

y. The war is personal. Even the crowds are made up of individuals. And our best, most effective, praying and prophesying and discipling and evangelizing is normally one-on-one. Whether in the alley or the door-front or across the coffee table, we need to see and love and care for the individual. God help us.

z. The war is urgent and intense. The Founder took every opportunity to press home the claims of Jesus Christ on individuals. He believed in hell and knew the consequences of failure better than most of us. He tried to optimize every opportunity to evangelize. For some, it will be the last opportunity they have to hear the gospel. Don't miss it. Grab it. Run hard with it ...

This alphabet of advice is priceless. May it be applied in your life and the lives of those you lead to advance the purposes of our Lord Jesus Christ in the great salvation war.

Major Stephen Court loves the Lord Jesus Christ and has served God with The Salvation Army in three countries over a couple of decades of officership along with his wife Major Danielle Strickland. The founding editor of Journal of Aggressive Christianity and the long-running Armybarmy blog, Court has published more than 20 books on topics such as holiness, evangelism, mission, prayer, leadership and more. He is currently engaged in mission strategy with the Army, looking to help the Southern California Division gain a spiritual foothold in every city (Every City campaign), and is passionate about multiplying Army bases composed of cell groups and Infinitum hubs (see infinitumlife.com).

Author Resources

Commissioner Joe Noland maintains a public presence online at themorerevolution.com. Noland has these book titles:

Lean Right, Love Left: Balancing the Body

Flight Manual for Prospective Angels

A Little Greatness

No Limits Together

High Counsel (with Stephen Court)

Out Of The Rubble… Revolution

Tsunami Of The Spirit (with Stephen Court)

9/11 On Our Watch (Twice)

The Holiness Dilemma: 7 Experiential Illuminations

The Salvation Singers: A God BEAT In Time

Double The Future: 6 Simple Saint-Making Strategies

Major Stephen Court is active on twitter (@StephenCourt) and has these book titles:

Proverbial Leadership (with Wesley Harris)

Be A Hero (with Wesley Campbell)

Revolution (with Aaron White)

The Uprising (with Olivia Munn)

One Day (with Jim Knaggs)

One Thing (with Jim Knaggs)

Holiness Incorporated (with Geoff Webb and Rowan Castle)

Salvationism 101 (with Danielle Strickland)

Boston Common (editor)

Hallmarks of The Salvation Army (with Henry Gariepy)

One Army [with Jim Knaggs, completing the One For All trilogy]

Greater Things (with James Thompson)

Army On Its Knees (with Janet Munn)

A Field For Exploits (with Eva Burrows)

High Counsel (with Joe Noland)

Boundless (with Danielle Strickland)

Tsunami Of The Spirit (with Joe Noland)

Blood And Fireworks (with Xander Coleman)

Warfare Prayer (with Janet Munn)

Leading The War (with Jim Knaggs)

Holy! (with Pete Brookshaw)

CPSIA information can be obtained at www.ICGtesting.com
Printed in the USA
LVOW10s1215100916

503986LV00004B/4/P

9 780865 440654